Three Months with

THE SPIRIT

THE SPIRIT

JUSTO L. GONZÁLEZ

ABINGDON PRESS
Nashville

THREE MONTHS WITH THE SPIRIT

Library of Congress Cataloging-in-Publication Data

Gonzalez, Justo L.
    [Tres meses en la escuela del espiritu. English]
    Three months with the Spirit / Justo L. Gonzalez.
        p. cm.—(Three months)
    ISBN 0-687-04599-1 (pbk. : alk. paper)
    1. Bible. N.T. Acts—Textbooks. I. Title. II. Series.

BS2625.55.G6613 2003
226.6'0071—dc21
                    2002155275

Originally published in Spanish as *Tres Meses en la escuela del Espíritu*.

03 04 05 06 07 08 09 10 11 12 – 10 9 8 7 6 5 4 3 2 1

MANUFACTURED IN THE UNITED STATES OF AMERICA

C ONTEN T S

INTRODUCTION

   This book is an invitation to study and to adventure. As a study it will require discipline. As an adventure, it will offer new panoramas and exciting challenges.
   Let us address discipline. Every important goal in life requires a discipline. If a young person wishes to become, for instance, a doctor or a lawyer, it will be necessary for him or her to follow from an early age a discipline of study and learning. If we are concerned about our physical health, we try to follow a discipline of exercise and nutrition. Athletes who prepare to compete in the Olympics must subject themselves to a rigid discipline for years on end. And yet, when it comes to spiritual life, very few Christians are willing to subject themselves to a discipline that will develop and strengthen it. With the excuse that we should "pray without ceasing," we do not set aside a particular time for prayer. And, since the Bible is always there, ready to be opened and read whenever we need it, we do not set a program of study. The result is that both our prayer and our knowledge of the Bible suffer, just as the body suffers when instead of following an ordered diet and a discipline of exercise we eat whatever strikes our fancy and exercise only when we feel like it.
   The first thing that we need in order to develop a discipline of study is to set aside a time and a place. The studies in this book follow a weekly rhythm: Each week there will be six short studies and a longer one. If you then follow this study privately, you will require at least half an hour a day for the six short studies and an hour for the longer one. Consider your weekly calendar and decide the best time for you to set aside for study. Once you have done this, make every possible effort to fulfill that commitment. Little by little, just as it happens with physical exercise, that study

rhythm will become more and more important for you, and the time will come when, if for some reason you are not able to follow it, you will feel its need.

If you are using this book as part of a Bible study group that gathers once a week, establish your rhythm of study so that the six shorter sessions take place on the days that you study in private, and the longer one on the day in which the group meets. On the other hand, do not be too idealistic regarding the time you have set aside for study. Life always has its unexpected interruptions, and therefore very few people are able to follow a discipline of study without interruption. Sooner or later the day will come when it will be impossible for you to study during the time that you have set aside. In that case, do not be disheartened. That very day, even if at another time, try to study the material assigned for it.

A place is almost as important as a time. To the extent possible, have a particular place where you normally do your private study. This will help you avoid distractions. It will also be a convenient place for you to keep your Bible, this book, your notebook of personal reflections, and any other material that you may find useful.

The next important point in developing a discipline of Bible study is the method one follows. There are many good methods for the study of Scripture. The one that we shall follow in this book consists of three fundamental steps: **See, Judge,** and **Act.**

However, before we discuss these three steps, there are two important elements that must be stressed, without which no Bible study can be productive: prayer and reflection.

At the very moment you begin each study, approach God in prayer. Ask that the Holy Spirit be with you during this study, helping you understand God's Word, and that the Spirit remain with you after you have completed the session, helping you to follow what you have decided. Always remember that, even though you seem to be by yourself, you are not alone; God is right there with you. It is not just a matter of you and your Bible, but rather of you, your Bible, and the Holy Spirit.

After a few minutes of prayer, devote some time to reflection, reviewing what you have studied before. In particular, remember those decisions you have made in previous days. Read your notebook. Evaluate what you have accomplished. Ask God for the strength to go forward.

Move then to the three steps of **seeing, judging,** and **acting.** As you will note, the material offered under each study is organized according to those three steps. The first, **seeing,** consists in examining the situation before you. In the case of these Bible studies, **seeing** will be examining the passage itself. What does it say? Why does it say it? Who are the main characters? What role do they play in the text? What is the context of what is said? In this first stage, we are not asking what the text might mean for ourselves, nor what it requires of us. We are only trying to understand the passage itself.

The second step, **judging,** consists in asking ourselves what the text might mean for us. Here, our personal experiences and our concrete situation become very important. We read the Bible in the light of those experiences and that situation, and ask what the Bible says about them. Therefore, when this book invites you to **judge,** it does not mean for us to judge the biblical text; it means rather for us to invite the text to help us judge our own life, situation, opportunities, and responsibilities. What does the text tell us about the church, about our faith, about our society? How does it affirm and support what we are doing and what we are? How does it question or correct it? What does the text call us to do or to be?

These first two steps lead to the third: **acting.** What we have seen in the biblical text, and the manner in which we judge how that text refers to our reality, require that we act in a specific manner. We study the Bible not out of curiosity, but in order to be more obedient to God's will. Therefore, the process is incomplete if we are content with seeing and judging. If we are to be obedient, we must act.

This **acting** can take many diverse forms, which depend both on the text and on our own situation. For instance, the study of a certain passage may lead us to greater commitment to the poor and needy in our community. The study of another passage may call us to witness to our fellow workers. And a third passage may call us to greater faithfulness in our participation in Christian worship. Furthermore, acting does not always imply physical activity. In some cases, acting may consist in a further prayer of repentance. In other cases, it may be abandoning a prejudice we have. Sometimes the action to be taken may be very concrete and brief—for instance, calling someone whom we may have offended. In other cases, it may be a long-term decision—for instance, taking up a different career. But what is always true is that, if we really study the Bible in a spirit of obedience, the Word that comes from God's mouth will not return empty, but will accomplish that for which it was sent (Isaiah 55:11).

Sometimes you will find that there are more suggestions for action than you can possibly follow. Take them simply as what they are: suggestions. Do not feel compelled to do whatever the book suggests. But do feel compelled to respond to your study of the Bible by an act of obedience—whatever that may be.

It is important to remember that we read and study the Bible not only to be *informed*, but also and above all to be *formed*. We read the Bible not so much to learn something, as to allow that something to shape our lives. Once again, the example of physical exercise fits the case. One who exercises lifts weights not only to see how much she or he can lift (that is, in order to be informed), but also and above all to become stronger, to be able to lift greater weight (that is, to be formed). Likewise, our purpose in these Bible studies should be not only to learn something, to know the Bible better, but also to allow the Bible to shape us, to make us more in accord with the will of our Creator.

This implies that the method of **seeing, judging**, and **acting** should be more like a circle than like a straight line. What this means is that **acting** improves our **seeing,** so that in fact the method could be described as **seeing, judging, acting, seeing, judging, acting**—on and on. Every Bible study that we complete, each action that we take, will make us better able to move on to the next study. Think about a traveler in a valley. In that valley, the traveler **sees** a dense forest, a road that climbs a hill, and the position of the sun. On the basis of what he **sees**, the traveler **judges** that he is not to try crossing through the forest, but that he is to follow the road. He also **judges,** on the basis of the position of the sun, in which direction he should go. Then he **acts**—begins walking. Eventually he finds himself atop the hill, where he **sees** new views that allow him to judge the direction to be followed and invite him to act in a way that he could not have guessed when he was in the valley. Therefore, his **acting** took him to a new way of **seeing**. The same will be true in a Bible study. If we make progress, we shall see ever wider views, and therefore not only will our seeing and judging lead us to a more faithful acting, but also our **acting** will clarify our **seeing** and **judging**.

What resources will you need to follow these studies? First of all, the Bible itself. Sometimes you will be tempted to shorten the time of study by not reading the Bible and reading only what this book says. The temptation will be even greater when the biblical passage is well known. It is important to resist that temptation. The purpose of this book is to help you in your study of the Bible, not to be a substitute for it. In the studies that follow, the Bible is quoted according to the New Revised Standard Version (NRSV). Therefore, if you use that version it will be easier to follow these studies. Naturally, if you have more time, you may wish to compare different versions in order to enrich your study. Some people following these studies have reported that they have used a Bible with large letters and wide margins, so they could write notes and comments. That is up to you.

Second, use this book. Try to follow the rhythm of studies suggested, reading and studying each passage on the day assigned. We are too used to living life in a hurry. Instead of cooking a roast for five hours, we place it in the microwave for thirty minutes. Sometimes we want to do the same with our spiritual life. If it is good for us to do one of these Bible studies a day, why not go ahead and do them all at once? Here again, the example of physical exercise may be useful. If you try to do a month's worth of exercise in a single day, the results will be very different than if you establish a rhythm of exercise and stick to it. Likewise, if we wish the Bible to shape us, to strengthen and to nourish our spiritual life, it is necessary for us to establish a rhythm that we can continue in the long run.

Third, you will need a notebook in which to write down your reflections, resolutions, and experiences. Write in it not only what is suggested in some of the studies in this book, but also anything that seems relevant to you. If something strikes your interest, but you cannot follow up on it at the time, make a note of it. Write your answers to the questions posed in the book. Make a note of your decisions, your doubts, your achievements, your failures. Use your notebook at the beginning of each study session, in the period set aside for reflection, to help you remember what you have learned and thought in the course of your three months "with the Spirit."

Make sure that every time you begin a study session you have at hand all of these resources: your Bible, this book, your notebook, and a pencil or pen.

No other resources are absolutely necessary for these studies. But if you wish to study Acts more deeply, there are other tools that you may find useful: (1) several versions of the Bible, in case you want to compare them; (2) a good commentary on Acts; (3) a dictionary of the Bible; (4) a biblical atlas. These resources will be particularly helpful if the seventh session of each week is a group study and you are responsible for leading the group.

Finally, do not forget two resources readily available to you that are absolutely indispensable for any good Bible study. The first is your own experience. Some of us have been told that when we study the Bible we should leave aside all our other concerns. Nothing could be further from the truth. The Bible is here to respond to our concerns, and therefore our experience and our situation in life help us understand the Bible and hear God's Word for us today. The second such resource is the community of faith. I have already pointed out that when you study the Bible you are not alone with your Bible; the Holy Spirit of God is also there. Now I must add that, in a very real sense, your faith community is also there. Acts was probably written to be read out loud, in the gathering of the church. Therefore, when you read it, even though you may be alone, keep in mind the community of faith that surrounds and upholds you. Read it not only as God's Word for you, but also as God's Word for the church. That is why this book includes the longer Bible study each week: to encourage readers to use it in study groups. These groups may gather once a week, but during the other six days you will each know that the rest of the group is studying the same Bible passage.

Again, this book is an invitation both to study and to adventure. On this last point, it is best to say no more. Adventures are best when they are unexpected and surprising. Plunge then into the study of Acts, knowing that at some point it will surprise you, but knowing and trusting also that, even in such surprises, God is already there ahead of you, waiting for you with open arms!

W E E K
ONE

First Day: Read Acts 1:1-3.

See: Acts is the continuation of the Gospel of Luke. In the first four verses of that Gospel, you will note that the book is addressed to a certain Theophilus. In today's reading we see that Acts is addressed to the same person. That is why Acts begins with the words "In the first book."

One could then say that Acts is the second part of a two-volume work. The first volume tells us about Jesus, and the second about the Holy Spirit. But the two are interwoven, for Acts tells us that Jesus gave his instructions "through the Holy Spirit." (Remember that in the Gospel of Luke, Jesus is born by action of the Spirit, so that now Jesus is giving his instructions through the same Spirit.) The Gospel of Luke speaks of Jesus, in whom the Spirit works. Acts tells us about the Spirit, through whom Jesus is made present. That is why this particular study of Acts is called *Three Months with the Spirit.*

Judge: When Luke wrote this book, he did not give it a title. The name of "Acts of the Apostles" was given by somebody else, probably in the second century, as a way to refer to this second book that Luke addressed to Theophilus. But the truth is that Acts is not so much about the apostles as it is about the Holy Spirit. In the first weeks of this study we shall see that the apostles are indeed central characters in the narrative. But already in chapter 6 these twelve move away from the center narrative, and eventually they disappear. Even Paul, who will soon occupy center stage, is not the main character of the story, for Luke does not even tell us what happened to him after he arrived at Rome.

The central character of the story is the Holy Spirit, who is present in the apostles and in the rest of the church. The purpose of the story is to lead us to understand how the Holy Spirit acts in the church, so that we may make allowance for such action in ourselves and in today's church.

Act: Make a commitment to read Acts with a new perspective, as the "acts of the Spirit." Pray, inviting the Spirit to act in you as the Spirit acted in those early Christians.

Second Day: Read Acts 1:4-8.

See: The passage deals with the promise of the Spirit and its power. But as part of that promise Jesus must clarify its purpose. The disciples wished to know if this was the time when Jesus would establish the Reign. But Jesus told them that they should not be concerned about this matter, for "it is not for you to know the times or periods that the Father has set by his own authority" (verse 7). That is to say that the matter of when the Reign would come, or when Jesus would return, was not their concern. It was not to that end that Jesus promised them the gift of the Spirit. Verse 8 begins with the word "But," which lets us know that Jesus was offering an alternative. The word "but" introduces the actual purpose of the promise of the Spirit, which is to provide the power to testify. No matter how eager the disciples may have been to know when all the things that Christians awaited would be fulfilled, their task was not to inquire about it. Their task was to be witnesses. And they would do this, not through their own power, but by the power of the Spirit.

Judge: It is important to understand this, for even today there are many Christians who think that if one has the Holy Spirit this should give one the clue to know, for instance, when the Lord will return. But the truth is that Jesus repeatedly told his disciples that such matters are beyond our reach. Today's text shows that our concern and our occupation are to be different: It is a matter not of knowing "the times or periods," but rather of being witnesses.

• Do you know someone who thinks that he or she knows when the promises of the end times will be fulfilled? Some such people claim to have that knowledge because the Holy Spirit has revealed it to them, or because they have discovered the key to unlock the meaning of Scripture in this regard.

• In the light of today's passage, what do you think Jesus would say about this?

Act: Make a decision that throughout this study your main purpose will be not curiosity, but rather obedience—above all, obedience in witnessing. Pray that God will help you in this purpose.

Third Day: Read Acts 1:9-12.

See: Compare this text with Luke 24:50-52. Note that Luke is the only one among the Gospel writers who carries the story of Jesus on to the Ascension.

Probably the most interesting detail in this passage is that, when the disciples seemed to be perplexed and looking at heaven, the two men in white robes confirmed the promise that Jesus would return. But in spite of that they told the disciples that what they were to do was not to remain there looking at the sky, but rather to go to Jerusalem. As a result, the disciples returned to Jerusalem, as Jesus had told them to (Acts 1:4, 8; Luke 24:49).

Judge: Note that the two men promised the disciples not that they would go to heaven but rather that Jesus would return to earth. Meanwhile, what the disciples were to do was to be faithful on earth. They were to go to Jerusalem, where Jesus told them that they should expect the gift of the Spirit. And eventually, from Jerusalem, they were to go "to the ends of the earth."

Christians have always had the tendency to remain static, "gazing up toward heaven," and forgetting about earth and what Jesus demands of us here and now. Using heaven as an excuse, some Christians have allowed great injustices without protesting in the name of their faith. Thus, for instance, during the conquest of the western hemisphere the original inhabitants of these lands were mistreated, exploited, even annihilated, and sometimes this was done with the excuse that their souls were being saved so that they could go to heaven.

But it is not necessary to go so far back in time. Similar attitudes exist even today among Christians of every nation and persuasion. They existed among the disciples, and if we are not careful, they will also exist in us.

Act: Have you ever been tempted to stand looking at heaven, where Jesus is, and forget the earth, where we are to be obedient? Reflect on that temptation and the shapes it takes, and write down your reflection.

Look around you, and ask yourself where is the "road to Jerusalem" where Jesus wishes you to begin your witnessing. Pray over it, discuss it with other people in your faith community, and write down your reflections and decisions.

Fourth Day: Read Acts 1:13-26.

See: The passage tells us of the election of someone to take the place vacated by Judas. With that end in mind, Peter established certain criteria or prerequisites that the person to be elected had to meet: It had to be someone who had been with Jesus from the beginning, "from the baptism of John until the day when he was taken up from us." Apparently, the group accepted this suggestion, and two people were named as possible candidates to take the place of Judas: Joseph Barsabbas, who was also known as Justus, and Matthias. Neither of these is mentioned anywhere else in the New Testament; therefore, all that is known about them is what this passage tells us. At any rate, they cast lots and this resulted in the naming of Matthias, who from that point on would be one of the Twelve.

Judge: When we study this passage, we are surprised because the requirements that Peter proposed for the person to be elected went beyond those met by many of the other eleven. In the Gospels we are told that Jesus called the disciples at various times in his ministry. Therefore, with the possible exception of the first four, the rest did not meet the requirements now established. As for being with Jesus "all the time," even Peter himself did not meet the requirement, for he deserted Jesus and fled. The same was true of all the others, except for John and the women who remained at the cross.

Do you know of instances in which, when it is time to name new leadership, requirements are set that did not exist before and that perhaps even the existing leadership does not meet? Could this be because the current leadership wants to manipulate and control?

Act: Think about the manner in which your church carries forth its mission in your neighborhood. Peter thought that since the original group contained twelve, they should forever be twelve. Is there a similar attitude in your church? Do your structures and procedures take changing situations into account? What sort of change may be required so your church can be more effective in mission?

Think and pray over this. Write down your ideas and conclusions. Make sure you discuss them with your pastor and other leaders in your church.

Fifth Day: Read Acts 2:1-13.

See: The events took place on the "day of Pentecost," a traditional Jewish festival. For that festival, people from many different countries had gathered in Jerusalem, and when the disciples who had received the Spirit spoke, the various people understood them, each in his or her own native tongue. Many were amazed by this understanding, but others scoffed, saying that those who spoke were drunk.

Note that the text underscores the unity of the followers of Jesus, saying that they were "all together in one place."

Note also the play on words (which exists also in the original Greek language) between the "tongues" of fire and the "tongues" that people spoke.

Note above all that the purpose of these different tongues is not to edify those who speak, but rather to make the witness about Jesus available to those whose mother tongues they are. Note finally that those who received the Spirit and spoke were not only the twelve, but also all those who were gathered, including women.

Judge: For today's meditation, center your attention on two subjects. The first is that what we saw earlier regarding the promise of the Holy Spirit is now fulfilled. Thanks to the power of the Spirit, the disciples become witnesses.

Second, notice that when the disciples received the Holy Spirit, people heard them, each in his or her own tongue. In order to listen and respond to the proclamation of the gospel, one did not have to understand the language of the first disciples, nor did one have to become like them. From its very birth at Pentecost, the church has been multilingual and multicultural. Sometimes, Christians in a majority or dominant culture think that others have to learn their language and culture, and to worship just as they do. At Pentecost, the Spirit did not reject the diversity of tongues in which the gospel is to be spoken and lived out, but rather accepted and even affirmed it.

Act: Ask yourself the following questions, and write down your reflections:

Do I give witness to Jesus Christ with the full fervor and strength of one who has received the Holy Spirit?

Do we love and support one another in church with all the love of those who have received the Holy Spirit?

How does my church reflect the fact that the Spirit makes it possible for people to listen in their own language and culture?

Sixth Day: Read Acts 2:14-21.

See: Peter's speech was a response to the mocking attitude of some. Although we generally imagine that they were laughing or scoffing at the disciples, the text does not necessarily say that. It rather seems to say that they were mocking the full event, the disciples as well as those who heard them in amazement.

Peter began by quoting words of Joel referring to "the last days." In other words, Peter was claiming that the last days had begun with the gift of the Holy Spirit and that ever since, we have been living in those last days, even though centuries have gone by.

What characterizes those last days, according to the quotation from Joel and to Peter's speech, is the gift of the Holy Spirit that undermines the distinctions of power and hierarchy that might otherwise exist. Thus, both the sons and the daughters shall prophesy, the young shall see visions, the elderly shall dream dreams, and even the slaves, both men and women, will receive the same power of the Spirit.

Judge: The society into which the church was born was much divided by inequality. Fathers had absolute authority over their children, even when the latter were fully grown. The elderly had authority over the young, men over women, masters over slaves, priests over the rest of the people. The gift of the Spirit, as interpreted by Peter on the basis of the words of Joel, questions all such hierarchies. Now the sons and daughters prophesy, and even the slaves have the same gift of the Spirit as anyone else.

In our society there are still inequalities. Sadly, sometimes we find in our own churches inequalities that we have learned or have copied from the surrounding society or even from the society of the first century.

Act: What relationship do you see between the gift of the Holy Spirit and the power to create a community that overcomes inequality? Is there any relationship between being such a community and having the power to testify?

Write down your reflections and share them with others.

Seventh Day: Read Acts 2:22-41.

See: This passage is the continuation of Peter's speech, which may be divided into three parts, each beginning with a direct address from Peter to his audience: "Men of Judea and all who live in Jerusalem" (verse 14); "You that are Israelites" (verse 22); "Fellow Israelites" (verse 29). What we are studying today are the second and third parts of that speech (verses 22-36), and the response of those who hear it (verses 37-41).

After interpreting what was taking place by means of the quotation from Joel, Peter moved to the center of his message, which was none other than Jesus Christ himself. What Peter said was known, at least in part, by his hearers. He said that his audience knew that Jesus of Nazareth was approved by God, as might be seen in the many miracles and wonders he did. His hearers already knew this. They also knew that they themselves plotted to destroy Jesus. What they did not know, and what Peter emphasized, was that all of this happened not simply because of their iniquity, but also because God so ordered it (verse 23). And what they knew even less was that in spite of all that was done to destroy Jesus, it did not succeed, for even death was not powerful enough to contain him. Following an argument on the basis of Psalm 110, Peter declared that Jesus rose again, and that "God has made him both Lord and Messiah" (verse 36).

It was in the midst of this speech that Peter explained, almost in passing, why the disciples acted as they did, when he said in verse 32: "of that all of us are witnesses." What this meant was not only that they saw it but also that now, by the power of the Spirit that had come upon them, they were witnessing (which is precisely what Jesus promised them in Acts 1:8).

The text turns then to the response of those who heard Peter's speech (verses 37-41). Even though that speech had been strong and even offensive, accusing them of having been part of the plot against Jesus, these people listened to Peter, and did repent. When they asked Peter what they were to do, he told them that they were to repent and be baptized. Then, as a consequence of the events of Pentecost, of Peter's speech, but above all of the power of the Spirit, thousands did repent and were baptized.

Judge: The first thing that surprises us when we come to this point in Peter's speech is that he claimed that his hearers were guilty of the death of Jesus. If we read the Gospel of Luke, that is, the first volume of this work in two volumes, we will see that not all Jews plotted to kill Jesus. On the contrary, it was the religious and political leaders, the high priests and the members of the council, who plotted to kill him. Furthermore, both in his Gospel and in Acts, Luke sets a marked contrast between the attitude of this religious and political elite and that of the people in general. The people were sympathetic toward Jesus and his disciples. The powerful were afraid to arrest Jesus in a public place, for they feared a riot on the part of the people. Further on in this study we shall see that the same was true with regard to the early church. The powerful and the members of the council sought to persecute and crush the disciples, but they did not dare for fear of the people.

Why then did Peter say that those who heard him were guilty of the death of Jesus? We have seen that these people came from different places, many of them quite far away. Given the social structure of Judea at the time, those Jews born and raised outside of Judea were looked at askance by those from Judea. They certainly were not part of the council, nor were they priests of the higher echelons. However, Peter said that they were part of the process that led to the death of Jesus.

This indicates that those who share power cannot hide behind their own lack of authority. If they agree to the plots of the powerful, if they do not oppose them, they too are guilty of whatever the powerful do.

There is an old Spanish proverb to the effect that one who kills a cow is not guiltier than the one who holds it down. Those who plotted and planned in order to take Jesus to the cross became guilty of his death. And those who simply accepted what the powerful were doing, and who at the end shouted "crucify him," and even those who simply went home without protesting, all made themselves guilty by what they did not do. (Which does not mean, as many have thought erroneously and with tragic consequences, that all Jews were guilty of the death of Jesus.) The guilt belonged to those who at that point allowed themselves to be used in the plot, or did not oppose it. It belonged also to the Roman authorities, who were the ones who actually crucified Jesus. And it belonged even to Peter, who simply denied Jesus and fled.

That is the first point to be taken into account when we consider this text. The second is the reaction of the audience. Upon reading Peter's harsh words, we expect those who listen will be incensed. They might even seek to kill him. That is what happens in other cases, both in the Gospels and in Acts. But something unexpected happens here. Those who heard Peter, rather than becoming enraged and attacking him, accepted what he said, repented, and were baptized. This unexpected result was the consequence of the main theme of this entire chapter: the presence and work of the Holy Spirit. Those who heard Peter believed him, not because his words were soft and convincing, but by the power of the Spirit. Peter said what the Spirit guided him to say, even though they might be harsh words. Since it was the Spirit who was acting, those who heard accepted what was being said. What does all this have to do with our present situation? The most important point is that one can be guilty of injustice without actively practicing it. Some people practice injustice actively. We do this, for instance, when we employ someone and pay less than a proper wage, or when we abuse our power over other people. But it is also possible to practice injustice, not actively, but simply by accepting it as if everything were all right. It is of this that Peter accuses his audience.

Act: Think about some particular injustice in your neighborhood or community. For instance, are there children who are not receiving an adequate education? Are there some people who do not have public services such as police protection? Is there unemployment? Choose any particular injustice. Describe it briefly in your notebook.

Now ask yourself what are the reasons for that injustice. Do you participate actively in it? If you do, think about what you can do to change the situation. If not, ask yourself if you do participate in some other way. (For instance, if the problem is the lack of adequate education, you could ask questions such as: Have you volunteered to help in the schools? Have you taken steps to improve the situation, perhaps writing letters or visiting the political leaders, or contacting the newspapers?) Remember that the Jews whom Peter accused had done no more than accept the injustice that was practiced against Jesus.

On the basis of the questions you have just posed, decide to take some concrete action against the injustice you have named.

Write down your reflections and decisions, and begin developing a strategy. Share your thoughts and decisions with other people, especially within the church community.

For Group Study

Begin the session by analyzing the text. Show that Peter's speech can be divided into three parts, and that what we are studying is the continuation of that speech as well as the response of the audience.

Ask the group to look for the word "witnesses" in the text. Ask how it relates to the promise that Jesus made in Acts 1:8. (Notice that this is Pentecost. The disciples have just received the Spirit. The very first thing they do is to become witnesses.)

In conversation with the group, pose the questions suggested above, under the heading of "Act." Try to lead the group to make some joint decisions.

End the session by posing the following question: Is it possible to be a witness without practicing justice?

W E E K
TWO

First Day: Read Acts 2:42-47.

See: The passage summarizes the way in which the early Christians lived. Verse 42 tells us that the disciples devoted themselves to four things: (1) the apostles' teaching, (2) fellowship, (3) the breaking of bread, and (4) the prayers. The rest of the passage explains more about each of these points.

Looking more carefully at the second point mentioned in verse 42, it is important to understand that the original meaning of the word translated here as "fellowship" was "sharing" or "having in common." Therefore, the practical expression of the fellowship mentioned in verse 42 is explained more fully in verses 44 and 45. Note that these two verses do not claim that the disciples went and sold all that they had and that they put it all in a common fund from which they lived until it was exhausted. What they say is rather that, precisely because they believed that everything was to be used for the common good, when someone had need, those who had properties or other goods would sell them in order to share with the needy. The text does not say they sold, rather that they used to sell or would sell; that is, it refers to an ongoing activity, and not to a single action.

Judge: One of the main attractions of the church in the early years was the love that existed among its members, and the spirit of sharing that flowed from that love.

That is why an ancient Christian writer says: "If we share in eternal things, how are we not to share in those that are perishing?" Think about your church. Is there within your own church community a spirit of sharing such that it witnesses to the love of

Christ and the love among you? Do you think that if believers loved one another more the world would be more inclined to believe?

Act: What do you have that is not really necessary, and that you could share with others who are in greater need? Write down your reflections. Pray over it. At the proper time, be ready to share.

Second Day: Read Acts 3:1-10.

See: The passage tells of a healing miracle that took place at the Temple. Peter and John meet a man who has been lame from birth, who is begging by one of the gates of the Temple. It is impossible to tell which of the Temple gates is here called "the Beautiful." It may be the gate of Nicanor, which was made of burnished brass and was therefore very beautiful.

The story is told with clear brevity. The lame man asks for alms. Peter tells him to look at John and himself. Most people giving alms will simply put a coin in the cup and keep on moving. Therefore, Peter's words would make the beggar think that he was about to receive more than usual.

What Peter then said would bring down any such hopes: "I have no silver or gold." But Peter continued. In declaring that he had no money, he did so not in order to rid himself of the beggar, but rather to give him something even greater: "in the name of Jesus Christ of Nazareth, stand up and walk." Then, following his words with action, he took the man by the hand and raised him up.

What is striking in this passage is the man's gratitude. His reaction was enthusiastic: leaping and praising God, he went into the Temple after those who had healed him (which would have reminded many of the prophecy in Isaiah 35:6: "Then the lame shall leap like a deer").

Judge: Think about all that God has done for you and for your loved ones. Is your gratitude like that of the lame man, leaping and telling everyone what has happened? Or are you rather an ungrateful person who simply accepts God's blessings as if you deserved them?

Act: Make a list of the blessings you have received from God in the last few days. Commit yourself to speak about them with someone, giving God the credit and the praise.

Third Day: Read Acts 3:11-26.

See: Yesterday we studied the healing of the lame man by the Temple gate. Today we shall study the speech in which Peter explained what took place. In that explanation, especially when we read it immediately after what we studied yesterday, two points stand out.

The first is that Peter did not heal the lame man so as to have an opportunity for preaching. Peter healed the man out of compassion, as Jesus would have done, with no ulterior motive.

The second is that when the opportunity offered, Peter explained the miracle, giving the glory to Jesus and making it clear that the miracle was not something he or John had done.

Note the contrast between this and the frequent cases today when people offer healing and other miracles either as a way to call attention to themselves or as a way to get people to listen to them.

Judge: Think about the good that you and your church do. (For instance, in the case of the church, think about its service to the community, literacy programs, child care, and so forth. In your own case, think about any good that you have done recently for another person.) On the basis of these actions, think about the following two questions:

1. Do I (or do we) do this above all out of compassion, or rather as a "bait" to bring people to church? If it is the latter, this is not true Christian compassion, nor is it what Peter shows in this story.

2. The other face of the same coin: After doing good, do we make use of the opportunities presented to us to explain that we do this in the name of Jesus and inspired by him? If we do not give such a witness when the opportunity offers, we are not being faithful witnesses to Jesus.

Act: In prayer, make a commitment to do something for another, without any purpose beyond the good deed itself. Decide that at a proper time you will explain your action as a result of your faith in Jesus. If possible, write down what you hope to do. When it is done, write down what actually took place.

Fourth Day: Read Acts 4:1-12.

See: While Peter and John were speaking, the representatives of the authorities came, arrested them, and took them to prison in order to be judged on the following day.

At that trial, the rulers and the representatives of the aristocracy in Israel gathered. The question posed to the accused was: "By what power or by what name did you do this?" What they were being asked was how had they dared to go to the Temple and heal someone there, having no authority to do so. Peter's response was firm and clear. What they had done, they did "by the name of Jesus Christ of Nazareth, whom you crucified, whom God raised from the dead." With these words, the accusation against Peter and John became an accusation against their judges for having plotted to crucify the Christ.

But there is more. If they did heal in the name of Jesus Christ, it is because that name is the only one in which what the apostles did could be done, "for there is no other name under heaven given among mortals by which we must be saved" (verse 12).

Judge: This passage is important because even today, among Christians, there are many who are still seeking salvation, at least in part, elsewhere. The first thing that some people do in the morning is to read their horoscope. There are those who seek meaning in life by amassing riches and honors. There are those who believe that the more power they have, the more valuable their life becomes. There are those who act as if they are closer to salvation by having more power or authority or recognition in the church. But all of these are false. None of them has the power to save, to give meaning to life. There is no other name under heaven, given to mortals, by which we may be saved.

Where do you find meaning for your life?

What was being debated in this trial was the matter of power and authority. The powerful were upset by the miracle. They were upset because the miracle threatened their own authority.

They were supposed to be the important ones in religious life, and now these Galilean upstarts came to do miracles in the very Temple of God! Therefore, what they asked the accused was in what name (that is, with what authority) they had healed the lame man.

Think: Are there in my church conflicts and debates over power? Are we perhaps like those members of the council who were more concerned about their power than about truth or the health of the lame man?

Act: If there is no other name by which we may be saved, make a decision that your life will center on your faith in Jesus and not on any other means of salvation. Write down some of the things that you find attractive, as if they were able to give meaning to your life. Decide to place them all in their proper place. If possible, share your thoughts and decisions with others.

Fifth Day: Read Acts 4:13-31.

See: In this passage we see Peter and John in two different contexts. First, we see them before the council of the religious leaders, hearing their verdict after Peter's speech. In that verdict, we see that the members of the council were astounded by the wisdom and the daring of Peter and John, and they then decided to order them to cease healing or teaching in the name of Jesus. When Peter told them that they could not possibly obey such an order, they simply threatened the apostles and let them go. (Note that the leaders were afraid of "the people" and that their decision reflected that fear.)

In the next scene, Peter and John told the rest of the church what had happened. One would expect that, given the order by the council and the danger of punishment, the church would ask God for protection against any further difficulties. But that was not what these Christians did. On the contrary, what they asked for was that there be more miracles and that they might be given power to continue preaching with boldness; that is, they asked for more of the same things that had caused their problem with the council!

Judge: Quite often in many of our churches we decide not to do something because it is "controversial." The only way in which

Peter and Paul could have avoided being called controversial would have been by ignoring the lame man. Today, the only way in which believers and the church can avoid controversy is by ignoring the needs of the world. If we seek to do some good this will always bother or disturb someone. This does not mean that we should seek controversy. That was not what Peter and John did. But it does mean that, upon seeing some human need, we are to respond to it, even though that response may be controversial or harm the interests of some.

Another common occurrence is that when Christian action leads to controversy, our natural inclination is to accept the existing situation in order to avoid further problems or controversies. However, this was not what the church in Acts did. On the contrary, it asked God for the power to continue along the same path, no matter what the cost.

What actions of love, charity, or justice should the church take today? Is it possible that we are not taking some of these actions for fear of controversy or opposition?

What would those early Christians say in such a case?

Act: Do you remember some time when you realized that there was some good you should do but did not do for fear of the way others might react? Do you remember some occasion when the church did the same? Think about those occasions and write down your reflections.

Sixth Day: Read Acts 4:32-35.

See: This brief passage is one of several summaries in which Luke tells us about the life of the church in general terms, in order to then give some concrete examples of what he first tells us in general. Tomorrow we shall see two of those examples. Today we shall look at the summary itself.

Note that the basis for all that is said here is the love binding the members of the community: "the whole group of those who believed were of one heart and soul." It was out of this love and unity, not out of an external obligation, that the practice described in the text developed.

That practice was quite simple: When someone in the community had a need, someone among the others whose condition was better went and sold a property and put the income from that sale at the disposal of the apostles, so that they would administer and distribute it. (The reference to "laying it at the apostles' feet" is a way of saying that they put it at their disposal.)

The result was twofold: On the one hand, there was no longer a needy person among them. On the other, that same spirit of sharing, and the love behind it, allowed the apostles to give witness "with great power," and the entire community to live in "great grace."

Judge: In many of our churches we do not talk much about money. When we do, we deal with the budget of the church and the need for people to contribute to that budget. It is during those stewardship campaigns that we are invited to think about what we have and how we use it. But seldom do we hear about the needs of other brothers and sisters, or about how we are to support one another, not just spiritually but also economically. Seldom are we invited to make an assessment of all that we have and of the need around us, in order to see how what we have may be used to meet those needs.

Act: In your notebook, make an inventory of all that you have. That may be a list of all your resources. Begin by listing material things, but also list other gifts, such as free time, education, and so forth. Then consider each of the items in your list as you ask in prayer: "How and with whom can I share this?" If at any point you believe that the Lord has answered your question, write that answer down. Decide to carry it through.

Seventh Day: Read Acts 4:36–5:11.

See: Luke now moves from his summary to two concrete examples illustrating what he has just told us. The first example is positive; the second is negative. The first, precisely because it is positive, does not need more elaboration, and Luke tells about it in very few words. The second needs greater detail. The first is the case of Barnabas; the second, that of Ananias and Sapphira.

Barnabas is one of the main characters in the New Testament. He appears both in Acts and in Paul's Epistles. The generosity that we see here we will also see later on, when Barnabas went to seek Paul in order to request his help in leading the church in Antioch. Barnabas also supported Paul, even though the latter eventually overshadowed him. It was that generosity that led him to sell a property and give the money to the apostles to be distributed among the needy.

On the other hand, the fact that his name is mentioned does not mean that what Barnabas did was extraordinary or unexpected. On the contrary, Luke has just told us that it was customary for the church to practice such liberality. Barnabas is simply mentioned as an example of what apparently other people were doing. This is also Luke's way of introducing a person who will be important later on in the narrative.

The second example begins with the word "but." This lets us know that what follows will contrast with the case of Barnabas. In a few words, what happens is that Ananias and Sapphira plot in order to sell a property, keep part of the money, and give the rest to the apostles, all the while giving the impression that they are actually donating the entire price of the sale. As Luke tells us, the consequences are tragic.

It is interesting to note that the word in verse 2 that the New Revised Standard Version translates as "kept back" is a fairly unusual verb. It is the same that appears in the Greek text of Joshua 7:1, where we are told that Achan took for himself something that ought to have been offered in sacrifice to God. Thus, what Luke is telling us is that the sin of Ananias and Sapphira was similar to the sin of Achan.

Note also that, as Peter told both Ananias and Sapphira, they had no obligation to sell the property, and once they had sold it they were free to keep as much of the money as they wished. Therefore, their sin was not simply in not having wished to share. Their sin was rather in the lie, in claiming that they were giving all when in fact they were giving only part. This sin was such that Peter told them that they had lied to the Holy Spirit. Their punishment was not for their having given more or less, but for the fact that, in lying to the church, they had lied to God. And that is a serious matter.

If we compare this with the case of Achan, we see how serious a matter it is. In saying that they had dedicated to the Lord the entire price of the property, Ananias and Sapphira were saying that the entire price belonged to the Lord. And then they kept part of it. What they had done in lying to the church was claiming that something had been consecrated to God and then holding it back. That is why, like Achan, they paid for their sin with their lives.

Judge: The theme of the entire passage (4:36–5:11) is money; but behind that theme and what Acts tells us about it, there is an entire way of seeing the church and its mission. What we are told here about money and its use is a consequence of Peter's Pentecost speech, telling us that we are now "in the last days." With the resurrection of Jesus and the gift of the Spirit, the last days had begun. Thanks to the gift of the Spirit, Christians lived in two spheres: the present sphere of sin and the coming sphere of God's reign. In that setting, the church had to be a sign of the coming reign. That is why the outpouring of the Spirit upon all, including sons and daughters, was a sign of the last days.

However, the reign of God is characterized above all by love, peace, abundance, and justice. Images of the reign that appear in the Old Testament underscore these elements of God's shalom. Therefore, when Luke speaks of the church as a community in which love ("the whole group of those who believed were of one heart and soul") was such that "no one claimed private owner-ship of any possessions," and that "there was not a needy person among them," he is describing not the life of an ideal community, but the life of a community that truly is a sign and a foretaste of the coming reign of God—as Peter would say, of a community that lives "in the last days." For us, it is a matter not of looking at the past, as if we were to reconstruct the ideal church of Acts, but rather of looking to the future, as those who seek to point toward the future community of the reign of God.

Commonality of goods is not an end in itself. The members of the church are called not to practice the commonality of goods, but rather to practice love. That is why it is not surprising that, even in a church that practiced the commonality of goods, Ananias and Sapphira were free to keep their property without selling it, or to sell it without giving the money to the apostles.

This is not the commonality born out of obligation or legislation, but rather one that is an expression of the love and the newness of life that is the gift of the Spirit.

Therefore, even apart from what we might think today about goods and their distribution, what is most important in this text is what it tells us about the nature of the church. In fact, this text illustrates what we have already seen—that the church is that community which, by virtue of the gift of the Spirit, lives in the last days even in the midst of this world that is still living in the old age.

According to Acts, the gravity of the sin of Ananias and Sapphira was not in selling or not selling, in giving or not giving. The sin resided in the lie. That lie was not only before the church, but also before God. Since, by virtue of the Holy Spirit, the church is the community of the last days, to lie to the church is to lie to God. Peter seemed to speak in terms of a great struggle between God and Satan. Satan had filled the heart of Ananias, who therefore had lied to the Spirit. Therefore, what Ananias and his wife did was not simply to keep a few pieces of silver or gold. What they did was to make way for Satan by lying to God.

If we take this passage seriously, it means that lying to the church is a very momentous matter, because it is impossible to lie to its members without lying to God. In the church the Holy Spirit is present. To lie to the church is to lie to God, and lying to God is not a light matter. It is, as Peter said, a satanic action.

If in our churches everyone who lies were to drop dead, there would be very few members left! Very few are truly candid within the church. Furthermore, one could even say that quite often the church is one of the places in which it is most difficult to tell the truth and be sincere. The tragedy is that we have lost the custom of speaking the truth. For instance, if we have doubts about some aspects of doctrine, seldom do we dare express them within a Sunday school class or ask others to help us with our doubt. If some sin or temptation eats away at our spiritual life, seldom do we dare confess it before the brothers and sisters. Even personal economic problems such as unemployment, lack of resources, and so forth are something that we hardly discuss within the community of the church.

The main reason it has become so difficult to speak the truth is that others don't speak it either. Since others don't speak of their doubts, mine seem exceptional. Since others don't speak of their sins, mine seem huge. Since others don't speak of their problems, mine must be my own fault. In other words, we lie to the church because within it appearances and lies have often taken the place of truth and love. What is most tragic about this situation, according to the story in Acts, is not merely that we thereby lose the consolation and support that others could offer. What is most tragic is that our hypocrisy and lack of candor open the way for Satan and deny the nature itself of the church. If the church itself lies, there is reason to wonder to what degree it is the church of the Holy Spirit.

In many churches today there is much talk about the presence and the gifts of the Spirit. That is good and proper. But too often we forget that the Spirit is to lead us to all truth (John 16:13), and that the highest of all the gifts of the Spirit is love (1 Corinthians 12:31–13:13). Quite often, while claiming that we have the Holy Spirit of God, we lie to one another by pretending to be holier than we are, to have more faith than we have, to make greater sacrifices than we make. Or we lie to one another with half-truths. Or we manipulate truth about brothers and sisters with whom we disagree, so that their opinion will not be taken seriously. According to the text, when we do such things we lie to the very Spirit of God. And what is worse is that the lie grows and grows, for because of our lying others do not dare speak the truth.

Act: Think about the ways in which you lie to the church. This does not have to be an explicit lie. Sometimes we lie by being silent or by our actions—for instance, we attend worship or Sunday school and there act as if we have no problems when in truth our heart is bleeding, or we act as if we had an absolutely certain faith when in fact we have serious doubts. Therefore ask yourself how, when, and why you lie to the church.

Decide that, at least within your own Bible study and prayer circle, you will speak the truth. (Naturally, this does not mean that you will be mean or cruel. It is not a matter of telling someone "you are stupid.") Above all, speak the truth about yourself and your life. If you have faith, say so. But if you have doubts, say that also. With your own example invite others to do likewise.

Think more specifically about money, which is the subject of the passage we are studying. Do you tell the truth to the church regarding your economic situation? Do you try to appear as if you have more than you actually have? Or on the other hand, do you try to appear as if you have less, so that you will not be asked for more? Decide to speak the truth also in this regard.

Write down your reflections and decisions. Pray, asking God to help you fulfill them.

For Group Study

Begin the session discussing what is said above about the meaning of the text and how serious a matter it is to lie to the church. Then pose two series of questions:

The first is the same sort of question we have asked above, under the heading of **Act:** How do we lie to the church? By making it appear that we have more faith than we actually do? More holiness? Fewer problems?

The second series of questions have to do with the church:

Why is it so difficult to speak the truth in some of our churches?

Could it be that we do not love one another as we ought?

Could it be that, even though sometimes we speak much about the Holy Spirit, we do not allow the Spirit to work among us?

What can we do in order to have our congregation be a place where one can really speak the truth in love?

W E E K
THREE

First Day: Read Acts 5:12-16.

See: This passage is another of the "summaries" that appear in Acts. These usually set a general theme or themes, which is further explained and illustrated by examples later on. This particular summary deals specifically with miracles. But it adds something that one should point out throughout these early chapters of Acts: In general, the "people" favored the new Christian movement. This situation will continue until we get to chapter 6, where new animosities will be aroused.

You may wish to take a biblical concordance and look up the word "people" in the first five chapters of Acts. Read the passages that describe the attitude of the people. See on which side they generally stood, either with the new Christian movement or against it. You will note that, up to the moment of the martyrdom of Stephen, the "people" favored the new movement. Those who opposed it were the high priests, the elders, the scribes, and the Sadducees—that is, the elite. Furthermore, on occasion the elite did not dare take action against the emerging movement for fear of the "people."

Judge: Do you think that today, at least in some cases, something similar happens? Follow this train of thought in two directions.

First, think about today's "elite"—that is, the people who form policy, values, and opinions. Think, for instance, about television and other mass media that are so powerful in our society. Do you find them supporting or opposing the church and its mission? Why do you think that is the case?

Second, and more important, think about the church itself. Are there situations in which the church does not get more involved with the common people because some of its leaders are afraid of the consequences? Is the church sometimes afraid of becoming identified with the "wrong" sort of people? Is this fear similar to that of the high priests, elders, scribes, and Sadducees of old? Is the church sometimes more concerned for its own prestige and for public opinion than for the preaching of the gospel?

Act: Now think about yourself and your own attitudes. Do you take the side of the "people," or are you also afraid that if the church becomes too involved with all the people, including the poor and the ignorant, it will lose its prestige and power?

Ask yourself: Who are the equivalent of the "people" today in your own town or neighborhood? How does your church relate to them?

Write down your reflections and share them with other members and leaders of the church.

Second Day: Read Acts 5:17-42.

See: This passage illustrates some of the points made in the summary we studied yesterday. While reading this passage, note that the conflict has to do much with public opinion—in other words, the opinion of the "people."

The story is fairly simple and clear. The leaders of Judea (the same ones who earlier had ordered Peter and John to preach no more) were "filled with jealousy," and as a result they had Peter and John arrested once again.

During the night, an angel freed the prisoners. However, they were freed not in order to allow them to escape, but rather so that they might go and continue preaching in the Temple. In the morning, when those who were preparing to try the apostles found the jail empty, they wondered what would be the outcome of these events. Then they learned that, rather than having fled, the apostles were still preaching in the Temple. The Temple guard was then ordered to arrest them, but they sought to do this "without violence for they were afraid of being stoned by the people."

Once again before the council, the apostles were tried on the basis of having been ordered not to preach in the name of Jesus. Peter responded by telling them that it was impossible to obey that order, since "we must obey God rather than any human authority" (verse 29). Then he took the opportunity to witness once again before the council: "We are witnesses to these things, and so is the Holy Spirit whom God has given to those who obey him" (verse 32).

Since the apostles had disobeyed the explicit order from the council, some wished to kill them. But one of the members of the council, Gamaliel, intervened. It was eventually decided to flog them and once again to order them not to speak in the name of Jesus.

Judge: We all know that we are to witness to Jesus Christ. What we often find surprising is how difficult it is to give such witness without provoking opposition and controversy. In the passage we are studying, the witness of the apostles led them to a strong confrontation with the religious leaders of Jerusalem. They were not seeking conflict. They simply healed the lame man and began teaching in the Temple. But those very actions, done without any thought of provoking conflict, soon resulted in jealousy, accusations, and even persecution.

Something similar happens today. Suppose, for instance, as Christians we decide we are to witness to Jesus Christ by providing drinking water in a neighborhood where it is not available. That is a good and worthy cause, and there would seem to be no reason to oppose it. But the moment we begin organizing for that action, someone will be upset. Perhaps it is the man who goes to that neighborhood twice a week with a tank full of water to sell. Or opposition may come from the political authorities who see in our plans to provide drinking water an implied criticism of their policies. Eventually, as was the case in the healing of the lame man, what we took to be an act of mercy becomes a motive of conflict and controversy. Suppose that then the mayor of the city or the president of the country calls us and "requests" that we give up such controversial activities, for "some important people" are becoming upset. What will we do? Will we know how to obey God rather than human beings? Or will we convince ourselves that, "for the good of the church," it is best to cease our efforts to bring water to that neighborhood? (This is not a purely hypothetical case, but something that has actually happened in our missionary efforts in another country.) Have you ever been in a situation in which you were pressed not to witness to Jesus Christ in order to avoid difficulties or conflicts? Who or what was pressuring you? How would Peter have responded?

Act: Think of a place or situation where you refrained from acting as a Christian in order to avoid difficulties. Pray over it. Write down your decision to witness in a similar place or situation as soon as the occasion offers. If possible, share your reflections with others.

Third Day: Read Acts 6:1-7.

See: This is the third example that Luke offers regarding the manner in which the church in Jerusalem dealt with economic matters. The first such example, short and positive, was that of Barnabas. The second one was the rather negative case of Ananias and Sapphira. This third example begins with a negative situation and shows the manner in which the church found a positive solution.

There were in Judea at that time two different cultural groups, the "Hellenists" and the "Hebrews." They were all Jewish, although one group was more closely related than the other to traditional Judean culture. The Hebrews were Jews from Palestine, who spoke Aramaic and who considered themselves more faithful and pure than the Hellenists. The latter were Jews who had been raised outside of Palestine, or those in Palestine who had very strong connections with other lands. They generally spoke Greek, and that is why they were called Hellenists. Both groups were represented in the early church.

As often happens in such cases, there began to be complaints to the effect that, in the distribution of the support of the church for poor widows, those belonging to one group did not receive as much as those of the other. Then the Twelve asked that a special committee be formed in order to manage the distribution of those resources. According to what the Twelve proposed, they would continue being in charge of preaching, while the new group of seven would be in charge of service to the needy (in this particular case, the widows). The congregation agreed and elected seven to form that committee. Acts gives us their names, and a remarkable fact is that all of those names are Greek rather than Jewish!

Judge: This episode presents one of the greatest challenges for the churches today: cultural diversity and how to deal with it. Here we have two groups, the Hebrews and the Hellenists. The Hebrews have been dominant until that point in the life of the church. The Twelve are Hebrews. But, thanks to the action of the Holy Spirit, the number of Hellenists has increased. Now there are complaints about the manner in which the resources of the church are being distributed, apparently favoring the Hebrew widows rather than the Hellenist ones.

This is a situation that is well known in many minority congregations. Many of them share buildings with a congregation of the dominant culture, and frequently the result is that there are complaints. In some of our multilingual or multicultural congregations, similar tensions and complaints arise. As in the case we are studying, what often happens is that those who have traditionally distributed and administered the resources of the church do not sufficiently understand the needs of other groups.

Act: Note the following guidelines as a model for action. Write down your reflections.

The Twelve heard and accepted the complaints of the excluded group. They did not wait until such complaints resulted in an open conflict. Is this how differences are handled in your church?

The church took the complaints seriously. It did not blame the widows of the Hellenists and acknowledged the need for change. Is this what happens in your church?

For that change, the church empowered those who until then had been marginal, by apparently naming seven Hellenists to distribute the resources. Is this a model ever followed in your church?

Share your thoughts with others in the church, and discuss if there are changes to be made.

Fourth Day: Read Acts 6:8-12.

See: Note the irony in this passage. The Twelve wished to have seven people named in order to manage the resources of the church, while they reserved the task of preaching for themselves (see verses 2-4). But immediately the text tells us that Stephen began preaching. Furthermore, the longest sermon in the entire book of Acts is Stephen's sermon, and he was not even supposed to be preaching!

In verse 9 the synagogues where the persecution was first organized are listed. The exact nature and number of those synagogues is not exactly clear, but it is clear that they were all Hellenistic synagogues. In other words, those who began the persecution against Hellenistic Christians were Hellenistic Jews rather than the more traditional Jews.

Judge: Those who began instigating the accusations against Stephen, and the ones who witnessed against him falsely, were Hellenists, just as he was. How do you explain this? What can it teach us?

(A clear possibility is that, since the Hellenists were already suspect in the eyes of the Hebrews, they were concerned that the fact that there was now Hellenistic leadership among Christians would bring further difficulties for all Hellenistic Jews. That made it necessary for them to make a clear statement that they were not like their fellow Hellenist Stephen. This is a well-known phenomenon in various minorities: some of the group are quick to dissociate themselves from those who are suspect to the existing structures of power.)

Then consider the following: The Twelve suggested that seven men should be elected. Does this mean that all officers of the church have to be men?

(A possible answer would be: No, since the Twelve also decided that they would reserve the task of preaching for themselves, and yet the Spirit clearly decided that Stephen would become a preacher and a martyr. The same Spirit who moved Stephen to preach even in spite of the plans of the Twelve can move the church to name women to its highest positions, even in spite of whatever decisions the Twelve made.)

Act: Look again at what you wrote yesterday in your notebook. Think about how today's study helps you understand the difficulties and injustices that you considered yesterday. Ask the Holy Spirit to show you what concrete steps you may take so that there will be greater justice and equality in your church. Write down your reflections.

Fifth Day: Read Acts 6:13–7:56.

See: According to Acts 6:14, Stephen was accused of two things: changing the customs (that is, contradicting the law of Moses) and speaking against the Temple. The same two charges had been earlier leveled against Jesus.

In his long speech before the council, Stephen responded to these two accusations. He did this by repeating the history of Israel, while emphasizing within that history certain elements that support his position.

First, regarding the accusation of rejecting Moses, Stephen tried to prove that it was not he, but rather his accusers, who actually rejected Moses. In order to make that point, he retold the history of Israel, pointing out that the leaders and the powerful repeatedly rejected those whom God had sent.

The first such case was that of Joseph, whom the Patriarchs, led by jealousy, sold into Egypt. But God had other plans, and that same Joseph whom they sold was later the instrument for their salvation. Moses had to flee Egypt because his fellow Israelites threatened to expose him before Egyptian authorities. But a few years later, it turned out that Moses was the one chosen by God to free the people (verse 30).

The point of this entire argument was clear in the following words: "It was this Moses whom they rejected . . . whom God now sent as both ruler and liberator" (verse 35). The same was true of so many other prophets that Stephen eventually asked: "Which of the prophets did your ancestors not persecute?" (verse 52).

Stephen then took his argument to its conclusion: What the ancients did with all those whom God had sent was exactly what the present leaders had done with Jesus, "the Righteous One," whose "betrayers and murderers" the leaders of Israel had become (verse 52).

As to the accusation of rejecting the Temple, Stephen did not deny it. On the contrary, he declared that "the Most High does not dwell in houses made with human hands" (verse 48).

The result of the entire speech was that the members of the council became enraged and decided to kill Stephen.

Judge: Why do you think that members of the council became enraged at Stephen's words? Remember that quite often, when something makes us really mad, the reason is not only that we do not like it, but also that deep down we fear that at least part of what is being said may be true. If someone says about us something that is utterly unbelievable, we pay no attention. But if the accusation is somewhat credible—and especially if we are accused of something we fear may come close to the truth—then we become furious. Could it be that the members of the council were enraged because they feared that in fact Stephen might be telling the truth, and they might be behaving like the ancients? Note also that such extreme rejections quite often are connected to self-interest. His brothers sold Joseph, the Israelites threatened Moses, and the ancients rejected the prophets because in each of those cases their own self-interest was threatened. In the case of the council, self-interests were connected to the Temple. The Temple was the basis of the power of the council. Without it, much of their power would disappear.

Think: When in our church someone is rejected and we claim we are rejecting the person because we are Christians, could it be that in fact we are doing something similar to what ancient council of Israel did? At least in some cases, it is quite possible.

Act: Think about someone in your own church who recently proposed something new, such as a different program or a new way of doing things, and was rejected. Then think again about what was proposed, taking into account the possibility that God might have been behind such a proposal. Or think about someone your congregation rejects or marginalizes. Why? Sometimes we say that we do this for moral reasons. But often we do it in order to protect our own prestige. If that is the case, we are acting like those members of the ancient council.

Write down your reflections. Discuss them with others. Consider the possibility of taking a different action or attitude regarding the issues that you have identified.

Sixth Day: Read Acts 7:57–8:3.

See: The council's fury led to violence. Members of the council covered their ears, which was a way of saying they refused to hear more. It was customary in Israel, when someone blasphemed, to cover one's ears and shout, in order not to hear the blasphemy. That was the reason they covered their ears in the council. But that very action was a way of not hearing what they did not like, not only because they considered it blasphemy, but also and above all because it uncovered their own disobedience.

It is in this story that Saul of Tarsus appears for the first time. Later he will become quite familiar as the apostle Paul. In this text, his participation in the death of Stephen was simply to acquiesce to it. But that attitude did not last long, for already in Acts 8:3 we are told that Saul was a leader in the persecution of Christians.

Note also the parallelism between Stephen's attitude at the moment of death and that of Jesus on the cross, both asking forgiveness for those who killed them.

Judge: The members of the council covered their ears. As we have seen, that was the prescribed action when someone was blaspheming, for it was thought that listening to such words made the listener guilty of blasphemy. But it was also a good way of not hearing what one did not wish to hear.

Today we do not cover our ears, for that is considered grossly impolite. But we still do the same with our attitude. When someone says something that we do not like, one of our most common attitudes is not to listen, as if we were covering our ears. Sometimes we don't like what is being said because it contradicts our opinions. At other times, we don't like it because it will require some action on our part that we are not ready to take (for instance, when someone is speaking of a great and urgent need and we choose not to listen). But in any case the result is the same: we do not hear.

Have you recently refused to listen to someone? Perhaps someone in church said something you did not like. Or perhaps someone came to tell you about problems and sorrows, and you did not listen as you should have.

Does someone refuse to listen to you or to your church? Sometimes even in the church the dominant majority refuses to listen to ethnic, cultural, or other minorities. Have you ever had such an experience?

Act: If during this reflection someone comes to mind whom you have refused to hear, write down that person's name. Ask yourself why you did not wish to listen. Write down those reasons, and in the very process of writing them down you will probably come to the conclusion that they are not as solid as you thought. Decide, as soon as you can, to approach that person and begin a conversation.

If in the course of your meditation you thought of some individual or group that has refused to listen to you, write their name or description. Try to think about why they did not wish to listen to you. Write down those reasons. Read verse 60 again. Ask God to forgive those who have thus offended you, and to help you forgive them.

Seventh Day: Read Acts 8:4-25.

See: Note that the main character in this entire chapter is another of the "seven" who were supposed to devote themselves to managing the resources of the church, and not preaching. In this case that person was Philip. Once again, the Holy Spirit took decisions of the leaders of the church and carried them far beyond what those leaders could have imagined or expected.

The narrative takes a new turn. As a result of the persecution that had been unleashed in Jerusalem after the death of Stephen, the witness of Christians expanded to other parts of Judea and Samaria. Generally, the outline promised in Acts 1:8 is being followed. (Read that verse.) Although the text deals with several matters, let us center our attention on Simon the magician and his story.

Few biblical characters have had as bad press as Simon the magician (also known as Simon Magus). In the ancient church it was said—and many history books still affirm—that practically every heresy that was circulating at the time whose origin was unknown could be traced back to Simon. During the Middle Ages, when reforming Christians rued the practice of buying and selling church positions, they called that practice "simony" after Simon the magician, who had sought to buy the gift of the Spirit. Not to be left behind, in the twentieth century Hollywood produced a film in which Simon Magus is a charlatan who tries to outdo the miracles of the apostles by means of tricks of magic. In general, Simon Magus is considered to be a hypocrite who tried to make use of the gospel for his own profit.

But the text does not say any such thing. It simply affirms that Simon believed and that he was amazed. It also says that Simon was a powerful man. He was so powerful that people spoke of him as "the power of God that is called Great" (verse 10). Simon, this powerful and prestigious man, was converted. But when he saw that the apostles had the power to confer the Holy Spirit, he also wished to receive that gift; and he wished to receive it in exchange for money. He had always been powerful, and now he wished to trade money—the symbol and the result of his power in Samaria—for the gift of the apostles, so as to be as powerful in the church as he was in Samaria.

It was to this pretension that Simon the fisherman responded with harsh words, telling Simon the magician he was "in the gall of bitterness and the chains of wickedness" (verse 23), and that therefore his money would perish with him. To this Simon the magician responded with what appear to be words of repentance.

When thus read, the text seems to be dealing not with issues of sincerity and hypocrisy, but rather with the matter of how power and prestige affect Christian life. Simon the magician was used to being powerful, and therefore it was difficult for him to see the difference between the power that he had in Samaritan society—money—and the power that counted in the church, the Holy Spirit. Simon Peter was a humble Galilean fisherman whom the grace of God and the power of the Spirit had turned into a fisher of people. Simon the magician, who was used to being called "the power of God that is called Great," could not therefore see the power of God as Simon the fisherman saw it at Pentecost, as the great leveler whose power was poured upon all people, male and female, young and old, powerful and powerless.

Then there was Philip. We are not told exactly what it was that he taught, nor are we told why after he baptized people it was necessary for Peter and John to lay their hands on the converts. The text does seem to imply, for whatever reason, that Philip did not make Simon the magician see the difference between the power of money and the power of God, between the power that makes people say of Simon that he is "the power of God that is called Great," and the power that makes Simon the fisherman an apostle of Jesus Christ.

Judge: The three main characters in this story—Simon the magician, Simon the fisherman, and Philip—describe the reality of many of our churches. Today many churches are living in a society where they seem to be increasingly marginalized. Whereas a few years ago the opinion of church leaders was often sought by public leaders before they made important decisions, that is no longer the case in many circumstances. A few years ago, it was expected that on Sunday morning almost everybody would be in church, and that is no longer the case. A few years ago, the media were always respectful of the church and its leaders, but not anymore. Therefore, many of our churches and many of our leaders are struggling with issues of relevance, prestige, and power.

It is at this point that today's text becomes particularly relevant. Sometimes we are so accustomed to being marginalized, to being ignored, that when a person of prestige joins us we are easily deluded into thinking that this somehow makes the church more relevant or better. Rather than challenging that person, as we would any other, to understand the contrast between the power that they have in society and the power of the Spirit, we act as if that person's power and prestige in society could and should directly and automatically be transferred into power and prestige in the church. Some churches boast that one of their members is a political leader, without realizing that thereby they are implying that this particular member is more important than all the rest.

At other times we similarly look up to famous athletes, rich people, and in some countries even dictators. Such a problem is neither new nor unique, for it already existed in the early church (see James 2:1-3). But the truth is that all of these things are manifestations of a power similar to that of Simon the magician, who has "no part or share in this" (Acts 8:21).

Over against that sort of power and prestige there is the power of Simon Peter, a humble fisherman who had difficulties understanding the message of Jesus, and who did not always follow through with his good intentions. But this other Simon discovered the presence of the Spirit and the power that gave him the courage to face the council of Israel, to face people such as Simon the magician, and eventually death itself. That power too is present today in our churches. As in the case of Simon the fisherman, quite often it is perceived most clearly by people who are quite powerless and lacking in prestige in society at large.

Then, someplace between the two Simons, there was Philip. The text does not tell us exactly what it was that he taught Simon the magician. But the narrative seems to indicate that, although he did preach the gospel to him, he did not clarify the contrast between the values of that gospel and the values of Samaritan society, between the power of the gospel and the power of Simon's money. Apparently, he preached to him and he baptized him, and went no further. And, though Simon followed him wherever he went, apparently Philip did not confront him with the tension between those two sorts of power.

People today are again tempted by similar situations. Although many of our churches have been marginalized in their own towns and communities, quite often people of prestige, money, and high social standing come to us. Many of them, not because they are evil but simply because they are used to it, expect that in church there will be the same deference shown to them as in the rest of society. Like the magician, they see no reason that their money, a symbol of their power in society, should not buy them particular respect in the church. At this point, it is important for us to remember that the gospel is also for them, and that perhaps in their case the good news of the gospel is that their real prestige and power do not depend on these things. Are we ready to present to them the radical demands of this gospel, or would we rather gloss over such things, for fear that they will be upset and leave?

Act: Consider the possibility that sometimes in church you have dealt with someone with particular deference because that person was powerful, prestigious, or rich. In that case, decide that from now on you will treat such persons just like the rest.

Make a decision. Be particularly mindful of the weak, the poor, and the overlooked in your community and church. Try to think of some concrete action that you may take in order to show them your respect and love. If at all possible, discuss and plan this with other people in the church.

For Group Study

Ask the group to discuss the following matters:

First, whether there is among us the temptation (or perhaps the practice) of giving special consideration to those who are rich, powerful, or prestigious. (For instance, do we give such people particular positions of leadership in the church over the rest?)

Second, how can we make sure that, at least within the community of faith, we treat all equally, not giving greater or lesser importance to people on the basis of their higher or lower position within society?

W E E K
FOUR

First Day: Read Acts 8:26-40.

See: The story is quite simple. Philip was in Samaria when he received a command from the Spirit to take the road leading from Jerusalem to Gaza. There he met a eunuch who was an important functionary in the queen's court in Ethiopia. He had gone to Jerusalem to worship, and now was on his way back to Ethiopia. Along the way, he was reading the prophet Isaiah, specifically chapter 53 (see Acts 8:32-33).

Led by the Spirit, Philip approached the eunuch's chariot and asked him if he could understand what he was reading. The eunuch told him that he could not understand it, and invited Philip to join him in the chariot, apparently so that he could explain the meaning of the passage. This was what Philip did, and beginning with the passage in Isaiah 53, announced the gospel to the eunuch.

The text does not tell us how long Philip traveled with the eunuch. It could have been just a few minutes. But, given the pace of travel then, it could also have been a matter of hours and even days.

At any rate, on hearing the witness and teaching of Philip, the eunuch was converted. Upon arriving at a place where there was water (perhaps a pond or an oasis on a road that was practically deserted), the eunuch asked Philip if there was any reason he could not be baptized in it. Philip responded that all he needed was to believe; and, when the eunuch declared that he did indeed believe, Philip baptized him.

Judge: The eunuch, by the mere fact of being such, could not be added to the house of Israel, for the law of Moses explicitly prohibited it. In spite of that, this Ethiopian eunuch had come to Jerusalem to worship. While others could be converted and accepted into Judaism, he could not. No matter how much he wished to join Israel, the fact that he was a eunuch precluded it. However, Philip was now telling him that nothing stood in the way of his being baptized, if he only believed. Since baptism is the act of incorporation into the people of God that is the church, what Philip was telling this man was that in the church the fact that he was a eunuch did not make him less worthy of admission than anyone else.

What this implies for the church today should be obvious. Unfortunately, there has always been a tendency in the church to exclude others for irrelevant reasons—or for reasons that would be relevant in other societies but not in the body of the redeemed.

In the past, in some of our churches people were excluded by reason of race. Today, although that is generally forbidden by the laws of most churches, there are still churches that practice such discrimination. Other churches and Christian communities discriminate on other bases.

What do you think Philip would have said to this?

Act: Discuss with other members of your church how it can show the surrounding community that all people, no matter what their condition or social standing, are welcome in your church.

Second Day: Read Acts 9:1-9.

See: Today's text is one of the most dramatic episodes in the Bible. An unexpected and radical change takes place in Saul. Up to this point, all that we know about him is that he was present at Stephen's death and that now he "was ravaging the church by entering house after house; dragging off both men and women" (Acts 8:3). If we were to read this story without knowing the outcome, we would expect Saul to be the villain in the story, which will probably deal with the long conflict between him and the recently born church and end with the victory of the latter. We even had a hint in that direction when we were told that, not being satisfied with persecuting Christians in Jerusalem, Saul was seeking ways to extend the persecution to Damascus.

But suddenly everything changes. When we least expect it—and when Saul least expects it—the Lord intervenes. Prideful Saul, who was "breathing threats and murder against the disciples of the Lord," and who was going to Damascus with letters of introduction, finds himself lying on the ground. There on the ground, he hears the Lord telling him that his enterprise is futile. Trembling and fearful, Saul surrenders to the Lord. Then he rises, blind and confused. He who until that moment had confounded and terrorized Christians! He who was certain and full of pride in his purpose, now needs to be led by the hand to Damascus. And to make things worse, now he needs to receive help from one of those hated Christians whom until that moment he had been persecuting!

Judge: Saul's conversion tears down all his reasons for pride. Quite often we think that conversion is simply "accepting the Lord." However, let us not forget true conversion is the death of the old self. What this means is that quite often, when we meet the Lord, no matter how sure we may have been about ourselves, we have to begin again like Saul, who gets up blind and needing help. (Remember the opposite case of Simon the magician, who thought that because he was important in Samaritan society he had a right to the same importance in the church.)

It is also important to note that Saul's conversion implies a call to serve God. God converts people not only so that they might become Christians, but also so they might serve the divine purposes. God has a plan for Saul. Saul has to go to Damascus in order to discover what the Lord wants him to do. Throughout the book of Acts, he will repeatedly discover what it is that God wants him to do.

Likewise, when God calls us, we are called to serve as God's instruments. Being a Christian requires not only a conversion, but also a vocation, a call to God's service. God did not call Saul and does not call us in order to warm pews in the church. God calls us for a purpose, a mission, a service to God, to the church, and to others.

Act: Think about the task to which God is calling you. There are various helps that you can have in seeking to discover that task, such as prayer, Bible study, the advice of others in the community of faith, and making an inventory of the gifts that you have received from God. Remember that, as in the case of Saul, what the Lord wants from you may be quite different from what you have imagined. Decide to explore all those possibilities. Jot down your reflections. Above all, do whatever it is that God is calling you to do.

Third Day: Read Acts 9:10-19.

See: The text now tells us that the Lord commanded a disciple in Damascus, Ananias, to visit Saul. God told him exactly where Saul was lodging, and how to find him. At first Ananias did not wish to go, for he knew that Paul was persecuting Christians and that he had come to Damascus with the same purpose. But the Lord insisted, telling him that there was a special mission for Paul: "For he is an instrument whom I have chosen to bring my name before Gentiles and kings and before the people of Israel." As a result, Ananias did find Paul. When Ananias laid his hands on Paul and prayed with him, Paul recovered his sight and was baptized. After regaining his strength, for he had neither eaten nor drunk anything for three days, Paul began preaching in the synagogues—the very synagogues where before he was planning to find supporters in seeking out Christians—proclaiming that Jesus is the Son of God.

Judge: Ananias was already a Christian before this story begins. For quite some time, he had looked from the church outward and had seen Saul "breathing threats and murder against the disciples of the Lord." Ananias was a Christian who therefore, when he heard of this Saul, was both afraid and disgusted. But Ananias was also a Christian whom God called to change that attitude, to accept the truth of the conversion of terrifying Saul, and to help Saul take his first steps in the Christian life.

A couple of days ago we thought about people whom the church despises as ancient society despised the eunuch, or whom the church does not welcome. We saw that the church must be inclusive and that, if it refuses to accept such people, it is actually refusing to accept the truth of the gospel. Today we see, in the case of Ananias, that when Christians respond to what God is doing in those other people, God may well surprise us. Ananias is not famous in the Bible. However, it was through him that God led Paul into the church, thus beginning a surprising ministry.

Ananias was afraid. He had good reason to be! But when he finally responded to the call, God made him part of a glorious history.

Act: Ask yourself: When we refuse to accept someone, are we motivated by fear, like Ananias? Or is there some other reason? If someone is converted and believes wholeheartedly, like the eunuch or like Paul, can the church raise objections and refuse to accept that person? Is there someone in our community to whom we should be going, as Ananias went to Saul? Perhaps God is preparing the path for us, as God did earlier for Ananias.

Write down your reflections and compare them with the reflections of others who are also following this study.

Fourth Day: Read Acts 9:20-25.

See: Immediately after his conversion, Saul began to preach Christ. He did this in the synagogues, among the very same people who used to see him as the champion in persecuting Christians.

The result was that some of these people saw him as their worst enemy. Now they were not as concerned about other Christians as they were about Paul. Therefore they began to plot his death. Saul learned of this but could not leave the city because his enemies were guarding the gates. (Remember that Damascus was a walled city.) But some members of his newly found Christian community helped him out of the city by lowering him in a basket from atop the wall.

Judge: Consider the reaction of the leaders of the synagogue when they learned of Saul's conversion. One might perhaps expect that now that one as prestigious as Saul had accepted Jesus, others among them would take the same step. But that was not what happened. On the contrary, those who earlier supported him in persecuting Christians now began persecuting him.

No matter how strange this might seem, it is not surprising. The leaders of the synagogue were more afraid of Saul than they were of other Christians, precisely because until recently he had been one of them.

There are two other important points for us today. The first is that, immediately after his conversion, Saul began to preach. When one accepts the Lord, the very first thing that one wishes to do is to share one's faith and joy. Just as conversion leads to a radical change in life, it also leads immediately to a desire to communicate the faith.

The second point is that these Christians helped one another. In planning to lower Saul from atop the wall, they were also taking a risk. Likewise, in today's church we need a solidarity that leads us to take risks and to make sacrifices for one another.

Now ask yourself: Do I witness to my faith everywhere, especially in those places where it may be risky to do so? And, does my church exhibit that solidarity and love that leads believers to take risks and to make sacrifices for one another?

Act: Think about your plans for the coming week. Consider your working hours, your leisure time, the time you are to spend with your family or with friends. Ask yourself how you can witness to Christ in each of those activities. Consider and confess the reasons you do not do it—for instance, in order not to be unpopular, not to offend, not to risk a friendship. Now consider how you can testify in such situations, while at the same time being respectful of others and their convictions. Write down the result of your reflections.

Think also about those in your congregation who need love and support. Probably there are some people in your church who feel trapped, as Saul was trapped in Damascus when his enemies were watching the city.

What can you do to help people out of such difficulties? If it is needful and useful, discuss this with others in your church.

Fifth Day: Read Acts 9:26-31.

See: When Saul went to Jerusalem, the disciples did not dare receive him for they remembered all the evil he had done, and they were afraid that it might all be a trap. But once again there was a believer who took the risk of receiving him. This was Barnabas, the same one who earlier sold a piece of property and brought the proceeds to the apostles.

In Jerusalem, we are told that Saul debated with the "Hellenists." As was explained when we studied Acts 6, the Hellenists were Jews who had been raised and educated outside of Palestine and who therefore tended to speak Greek rather than Aramaic. Paul himself was a Hellenist. So were Stephen and the rest of the seven who were chosen to administer the resources of the church. Therefore, if Saul was debating with such Hellenists, he was debating with a group he knew quite well. As we saw earlier, it was Hellenistic synagogues that began the persecution against Stephen, also a Hellenist.

The reason these Hellenists sought to kill Saul is clear. They were already looked at askance by the "Hebrews"—that is, by Jews who were natives of Palestine. The fact that now some Hellenists had decided to become Christians would surely lead to more prejudice against them. Therefore, the Hellenists were interested in showing that they had nothing to do with the new sect, and they did this by persecuting it.

Note that in many ways the attitude of the disciples in Jerusalem when they learned of the conversion of Saul was similar to that of Ananias when he was first told to go see Saul, and even to that of those who decided to persecute him. It is always quite easy to label others and quite difficult to think that they might really change. Note also that once again, as in Damascus, the believers in Jerusalem eventually helped Saul leave the city and go to Tarsus.

Judge: The Christian community has been rent by controversies over the centuries. Some of these controversies have been very bitter, even violent. Therefore, it is not surprising that sometimes individuals and even entire denominations hold grudges against others and do not trust them. This is still true in the Latino community that I know best, where there are Protestants who will have nothing to do with Roman Catholics. But it is also true in other communities. Some of us refuse to relate to Christians of other denominations either because they are too "liberal" or too "conservative." Also, although we do not confess it even to ourselves, we hold prejudices against other Christians and denominations for reasons of class and culture. Sometimes we criticize other churches and other styles of worship for being "uncouth." What we really mean is that we do not wish to be confused with them for fear that people will think that we too are uncouth. Other times we criticize those whose worship is too traditional, saying even that it is "cold" or "irrelevant." When we do this—though we do not confess it to ourselves—we are also acting out of a fear that we ourselves might be considered cold or irrelevant.

In all these cases, what we are doing is refusing to admit as brothers and sisters those whose opinions we do not agree with, or whose history we find questionable. We are then very similar to those Hellenists who tried to distance themselves from Hellenistic Christians, to the point of persecuting them. Or if not, we may be similar to those early Hebrew disciples who were not ready to accept Paul because of his past history.

Do you or does your church ever behave along these two lines?

Act: Think about the community within a radius of five or six miles of your church. Are there some in this neighborhood who should be in your church but who are not there because they are not sure they will be well received? Think of people of a different ethnic background, a different culture, or a different social class than those dominant in your church. Consider what steps must be taken in order to make it clear to them that yours is a welcoming church. Discuss these steps with others, and take them.

Think also about other churches in your community with whom your own denomination differs. What can be done in order to promote unity and respect among all churches and Christians?

Sixth Day: Read Acts 9:32-43.

See: After several chapters dealing with the mission among the Hellenists, having to do first with the election of the seven, then with the ministries of Stephen and Philip, and finally with Saul, Acts comes back once again to Peter and his preaching. Peter is now traveling through Judea, and here we are told of two miracles that take place through his ministry. The first is the healing of Aeneas and the second the raising of Dorcas. It is interesting to note that here we have a case of something that Luke does quite frequently in his Gospel: He joins a story about a man and another about a woman. The man is Aeneas, and the woman is Dorcas, whose name means gazelle and is translated in Aramaic as Tabitha.

Note that the purpose of these two miracles is not publicity. On the contrary, in the case of Dorcas, Peter asks all to leave the room. If people throughout the area hear about it, this is a secondary result of the miracle; the fundamental purpose is not to impress people but rather to heal Aeneas and to raise Dorcas.

Judge: The book of Acts is full of miracle stories, to such a degree that it is impossible to study it without having to face the question of miracles. Since here we are dealing with two parallel miracles, this seems to be an appropriate time to consider the entire matter of miracles.

The main reason we sometimes have problems with miracle stories is that we have been taught to understand the world in such a way that there is no place in it for miracles. According to the modern worldview, the world is a closed system of causes and effects that can be explained by mechanistic principles. In this view, even phenomena we cannot explain at present could be explained were it not for our ignorance. Such a universe is entirely closed to any divine intervention and functions only on the basis of inalterable laws that cannot be overruled by other powers.

But the truth is that this is not the only way to understand the world. Nor is it a purely objective view. Such a mechanistic view, which excludes divine or other intervention, serves the interests of the status quo and holds particular attraction for those whose position in the world and in society is such that any radical change would be seen as negative. It also tends to discourage those whose position in the world is such that their hopes lie in a radical and perhaps even unexplainable change. If all that will be results from what already is, there is no reason to hope for a new order. Without such hope, every struggle and every resistance against injustice lose impetus. Thus, our modern mechanistic view plays a practical role similar to that of the Sadducees and the other members of the council, who wished to know by what name or which authority the apostles had dared break the existing order. However, for those whose only hope is a radical change, a new thing, an intervention from on high, the closed and mechanistic worldview is merely one more burden added to the weight of their oppression.

That is one reason that many in ethnic minority churches, as well as many among the poor, have always believed in an active God and in a world that is open to the action of such a God. God is creator of heaven and earth. The earth, the world such as it already is, with all its physical laws, is indeed God's creation. But this earth is not all that God has created and rules. God is also creator and ruler of "heaven," of what we do not see, of the mystery that intervenes in this "earth" of established orders and predictable effects. The miracles in Acts, far from turning this book into a distant and impenetrable document, bring us closer to it, for today's church must live precisely by faith and trust in a God who does intervene in our lives and our history.

Act: In spite of all that leads us to think otherwise, look at the world as a reality open to divine intervention. This does not mean that we are to act as if there were no order in the universe. What it does mean is that we are to live in expectation as those who truly expect from God great and even unimagined things. Ask God to help you live in that way. Particularly, ask God that in times of anxiety and desperation you may be able to trust God's grace and power. The world is not closed to divine intervention. Make sure that you are not closed to it.

Seventh Day: Read Acts 10:1-48.

See: The story begins in two different places. Cornelius the centurion is in Caesarea. Peter is lodging in Joppa, in the house of Simon the tanner.

In Caesarea, Cornelius has a clear vision telling him that he is to send for Peter, and giving him exact directions as to how to find the apostle. In response to that vision, Cornelius sends messengers to Joppa in search of Peter.

In Joppa, Peter also has a vision, but it is not clear at all. He sees "something like a large sheet" coming down from heaven with all kinds of animals. He also hears a voice that orders him to kill and eat. Since some of the animals are unclean, Peter refuses. But the voice insists, inviting him three times to eat, and declaring that "what God has made clean, you must not call profane." Then the sheet returns to heaven. Peter is confused and puzzled about the meaning of this vision when Cornelius's messengers arrive. The next day Peter, the messengers, and some others from among the believers in Joppa leave for Caesarea.

On arriving in Caesarea, Peter finds Cornelius expecting him; he has even gathered a group to hear what Peter has to say. Cornelius tells Peter about his vision. The apostle comes to the conclusion that "God shows no partiality, but in every nation anyone who fears him and does what is right is acceptable to him," and begins preaching to those gathered.

While Peter is preaching, Cornelius and his guests receive the Holy Spirit. This is a surprise to the Jewish Christians present, who marvel that such a thing might happen among Gentiles. But Peter, possibly connecting all of this with the vision he received earlier, and which now he begins to understand, orders that they be baptized.

The story of Peter and Cornelius shows the Spirit acting in surprising ways. Peter was one of the earliest disciples of Jesus and one of his most faithful followers. He apparently was a leader among the Twelve. Cornelius was a pagan who feared God—that is to say, while believing the teaching of Judaism, he was not quite ready to become a convert. Peter was a member of the inner circle; Cornelius was an outsider.

But something quite unexpected happened. Peter, the disciple, had a confused and puzzling vision, which he himself did not understand. Cornelius, the Roman pagan centurion, received a clear vision, which even gave him the address of the place where Peter was dwelling.

When the two met, Cornelius learned much. He learned about Jesus, and he was converted and baptized. But Peter also learned much. He learned that "God shows no partiality." On the basis of what he had now learned, when Cornelius and his guests gave signs that they had received the Holy Spirit, Peter decided to baptize them. And, if we were to continue reading the story into chapter 11, we would see that eventually the church in Jerusalem also would learn much.

In this study of Acts we have repeatedly found the Holy Spirit adding unexpected people to the church. One of them was the Ethiopian eunuch, who for reason of his physical condition could not be added to the people of God. Another was Saul, who until that very moment had been persecuting Christians. Now there is this Cornelius, a centurion in the Roman army—precisely the army that many considered an oppressive force and that had crucified Jesus. But in today's passage, even more than in those other stories, we see something that we often forget: that adding such people to the church is beneficial not only to them but also to the church itself, which grows spiritually. In this case, Peter could understand more fully that "God shows no partiality," and this led him to a new sense of mission.

Judge: The same is true in our case. When new people are added to the church, we discover new dimensions to the Bible, our faith is strengthened, and our zeal increases. That is why, when we do not open the way for such persons and do not welcome them, we lose something beyond their mere presence.

Think about your own church. When were the last people added? When were people added who did not belong to the church at all? Probably, if it has been a long time since your church has received such people, vitality and enthusiasm are also waning. If you frequently receive new believers, your church will grow in vitality and enthusiasm. Those who come into the church from outside bring with them the gift of new life and new vision.

Consider the following proposition: The story of Peter and Cornelius is not only about the conversion of Cornelius, but also about the conversion of Peter. What can one mean when speaking here of the "conversion of Peter"?

Act: Think about some of the people who have been added to your church more recently. Ask yourself what you can learn from them, as well as what the church at large can learn. Make sure that you give them opportunity to talk to you and to express themselves, so that you as well as the church can hear what they have to say. If your church does not have ways to let such new people be heard, think about ways in which that situation can be changed.

For Group Study

Review with the group the studies of the last few days. During this week we have studied about the eunuch, about Paul after his conversion, and about various individuals and groups that the church excludes, or at least whom it does not welcome enthusiastically. We also spoke of Christians who welcome one another. Ask the group to try to remember what groups, what sort of people, were brought to mind in those earlier studies. As the group names such people, list them on newsprint.

Having made such a list, ask the group:

What do we miss when these people are not part of our community?

What can we learn from them?

What can we do to let them know that the gospel and the church are also for them?

Lead the group in a discussion of these matters. At the end, remind the group that exactly what we shall learn from such people we will not know until they themselves tell and teach us.

W E E K
FIVE

First Day: Read Acts 11:1-18.

See: The story continues what we studied yesterday. If it was difficult for Peter to understand and accept his own vision, how much more difficult would it be for those who were back at the church in Jerusalem! That is why the author tells us that "when Peter went up to Jerusalem, the circumcised believers criticized him" (verse 2).

Responding to such criticism, Peter tells them about his vision and what happened at the home of Cornelius. It is then that the church in Jerusalem comes to the conclusion that "God has given even to the Gentiles the repentance that leads to life" (verse 18).

Judge: In yesterday's study we concluded that it is possible to speak not only of the conversion of Cornelius, but also of the conversion of Peter. In today's study, we come to a place of which it is possible to speak also of the conversion of the church in Jerusalem. It was thanks to the conversion of Cornelius that the believers in Jerusalem now became more fully aware of the scope of the gospel, which was not only for Jews but also for Gentiles.

Try to imagine the rest of the book of Acts without the conversion of the eunuch, without the conversion of Saul, without Peter coming to the conclusion that "God shows no partiality," and without the church in Jerusalem learning that "God has given even to the Gentiles the repentance that leads to life." Most of the rest of the book would have to be eliminated, for it deals with Paul's mission. Without the lesson that the church learned through those conversions, there would have been no mission to the Gentiles. Christianity would have been no more than a Jewish sect, and most of us would never have had the opportunity to hear the gospel. All of this depended on the church being able to learn from such unexpected additions to it.

Likewise, can we even imagine what we are losing whenever we close the doors of the church to other equally unexpected people? Could there be someone among them in whom the Spirit is already acting, as the Spirit acted in Cornelius, and who is only awaiting our witness in order to accept the gospel and thereby to enrich our life as a church? We know not, and therefore we must always be ready to witness to all, to welcome all.

Act: Look back at your notes and thoughts of yesterday. Have you acted today according to what you decided then? If you have, write down the result. If not, consider and write down the reasons.

Second Day: Read Acts 11:19-30.

See: Up to this point, Acts has dealt almost exclusively with the church in Jerusalem and its direct mission. The main exception was chapter 8, which dealt with the mission of Philip in Samaria. Now the center of action will shift. Although Jerusalem will still be important and we will occasionally hear of the church in that city, attention now centers on the recently founded church in Antioch, and eventually will shift even further to the missionary work coming out of that church.

The text tells us first of all of the origin of that church, which was due to some Christians who left Jerusalem because of the persecution and went about proclaiming the message of Jesus. Some of them, from Cyprus and Cyrene, eventually reached Antioch, where they began doing something new: They began preaching among the Gentiles. The cases of Gentile converts that we have seen so far are relatively isolated, such as that of the Ethiopian and that of Cornelius. But here in Antioch a new policy was inaugurated, preaching to those who were not Jews.

The result was double: the church in Antioch grew, and in Jerusalem some began worrying about what was happening in Antioch. Therefore they sent Barnabas, who upon arrival rejoiced at what was taking place there and, one would imagine, sent positive reports to Jerusalem. From that point on, Antioch seems to have become the normal place of residence for Barnabas, who sought to strengthen the church in that city. To that end he went to Tarsus looking for Paul and brought him to Antioch in order to help him. It was there that the Gentile world began taking cognizance of the existence of the new faith and therefore began giving its followers the name of "Christians."

Some time later, a prophet announced that there would be a great famine, and the younger church in Antioch decided to send support to the needy in Judea. Barnabas and Saul went to Jerusalem, the main city in Judea, to take the offering from Antioch. Upon their return, they brought with them John Mark, who would later accompany them on their first missionary journey.

Judge: The church has always grown through mission. In that mission, younger churches have been founded. As a result, we have often grown accustomed to the notion that the younger and perhaps smaller churches are dependent on the older and larger ones and that they will remain so for a long time. Sometimes the result is that the younger churches are taught to be dependent, to be recipients rather than agents of mission. Another result is that the older churches think that they will always be sending and giving. A clear case of this we see in the criticism, often leveled against some of our denominations, that we are no longer sending as many missionaries as we used to. Such criticism implies that the churches that were founded by earlier missionaries are not self-sufficient and self-propagating; that somehow they still need us and our missionaries to guide them, to give witness in their own lands.

But even more seriously, the result of such a view is that the churches that have traditionally sent missionaries, the older, more established, and usually more affluent churches, do not realize how much they have to learn from the churches they founded a generation or two ago. We forget that, as in the case of Jerusalem and Antioch, mission is a two-way street. The churches that we founded may have something important to contribute to us today, and if we do not receive it and do not listen to them, we may be all the poorer.

Act: Think about the church in your nation and overseas. Are there churches in faraway places that your national denomination founded or helped found? What is your church doing in order to learn from them, to receive from them whatever they may have to contribute to you? Pose that question to the committee or group in your own local congregation that is in charge of missions.

Third Day: Read Acts 12:1-3.

See: The passage is brief but says much. Persecution grows worse. Up to this point, those who had persecuted Christians were the religious leaders of Judaism. By and large, Roman authorities had stood on the sidelines—although it was they who crucified Jesus. Now, with the intervention of Herod, the situation worsened. Although Herod was a Jew, he was also a Roman officer, placed and sustained in his position of authority by Roman power. If Herod began persecuting Christians, this meant that Roman authorities, at least in Palestine, had decided to follow the example of the religious authorities and persecute Christianity. Verse 3 hints that Herod did this in order to cater to the Jewish leadership. At some point later, we shall see Paul making use of Roman authority as a protection against persecution coming from some Jewish quarters. For the time being, however, and certainly within Judea, all that Christians can expect from Romans is greater opposition.

Judge: There were many causes for the early persecution of Christians. In the case of the leaders of the council, we have already noticed that these causes included the manner in which Christianity seemed to threaten their authority. Later on, in chapter 19, we shall see that persecution also had economic causes. Here we see persecution for political reasons. Herod knew that he was not very popular among the Jewish leadership and that his right to occupy the throne of Judea was at best questionable. Therefore, in order to strengthen his position, he attacked Christians. It is important to note that Luke, in writing Acts, takes into account these various realities impinging on the life of the church.

Do we understand those realities today and how they affect the life and mission of the church?

If a politician approaches us and tells us something we like, are we conscious of the agendas that may be behind such words?

When we seek to improve living conditions, be it in our own neighborhood or some place else in the world, do we understand the economic and other interests that will support us, as well as those others that will oppose us, and why they will do so?

Act: Think about your own church and neighborhood. Besides the church, what other institutions and interests are present in your neighborhood? Which support the work and mission of the church? Which do not? Write down your reflections and add more details in the following days as you become aware of other realities and issues in this connection. If others are following the same study, compare your reflections with them and together think about how this will affect the mission of the church.

Fourth Day: Read Acts 12:4-19.

See: The references to the Festival of Unleavened Bread and the Passover in verses 3 and 4 explain why Peter was not tried and condemned immediately. Herod was waiting for the religious festivities to be over. Perhaps he wished to make certain that, the festivities having finished, the trial and death of Peter would be the center of public attention, and that the pilgrims who had come to Jerusalem for the religious celebrations would return to their countries telling how zealously Herod defended Jewish orthodoxy.

Herod took all sorts of precautions to keep Peter from escaping. Having groups of four soldiers was customary in the Roman army; such a group took turns at each guard position, each individual keeping guard for three hours at a time. Herod assigned four such squads, a total of sixteen men, to guard Peter. Then, for greater security, Peter was tied by a chain to a soldier on each side.

But there is another power at work. The church is fervently praying for Peter. The night before the trial, an angel came to the prison and freed Peter. That liberation was so miraculous that not even the church itself was ready to believe it, in spite of its prayers—as the author tells us in a narrative that is not lacking in humor.

Almost in passing, Acts mentions James and others whom Herod killed or mistreated. It is important, before we center our attention on Peter's liberation, to note that here we have two parallel stories of two apostles: James and Peter. One dies; the other is freed. We are not told that one had more faith than the other. One can also imagine that after the arrest of James the church was praying for him as fervently as it did later for Peter.

Judge: It is important to remember this, for there is a commonly held notion that if one has faith all problems will be solved and things will turn out as one wishes. When some are ill and are not healed in spite of prayer, there are those who say that it is because they did not have faith. If someone dares a difficult act of witnessing in dangerous circumstances, and dies because of it, even then there are those who say that it was because of a lack of faith.

The Bible certainly says that God can free, and sometimes does free, people. The Bible also says that lack of faith leads to punishment, both in the present and in the future. But the Bible also says that not always does faith lead to the most pleasant result, and that there are even cases when faith, rather than making us suffer less, increases our difficulties and suffering. This may be seen in Hebrews 11:3-38. There we are told first of those who through faith witnessed great miracles and attained significant victories. These were those "who through faith conquered kingdoms, administered justice, obtained promises, shut the mouths of lions, quenched raging fire, escaped the edge of the sword, won strength out of weakness, became mighty in war, put foreign armies to flight" (Hebrews 11:33-34). But we are also told of "others" who through the same faith obtained exactly the opposite result (see Hebrews 11:35-38).

Today's passage is an example of the same diversity of results. Because of their faith, James died and Peter was freed. This does not at all mean that James had less faith than Peter or that the church prayed better for Peter than it did for James, or that the preaching of James offended Herod more than did that of Peter. In fact, there are strong and historical indications that eventually Peter died for his faith too.

On that occasion God freed Peter and thus showed God's power and design; slightly over twenty years later, God did not free him, and that also showed God's power and design. Christians should never forget that at the very center of our faith stands the cross of Jesus, who suffers, not because he lacks faith or because he is sinful, but for exactly the opposite reason.

Act: Pray for more faith—not faith that will make everything turn out as you wish, but rather faith to see the action of God both when things turn out as you would like, and when they do not. Write down your prayer and return to it as often as necessary.

Fifth Day: Read Acts 12:20-24.

See: The exact nature of the dispute of Herod with Tyre and Sidon is not known. It apparently had to do with economic competition, and finally the two cities sued for peace because they needed the wheat from Judea. At any rate, Herod decided to celebrate his triumph at a great feast. There his sycophants came to the point of saying that when Herod spoke it was with a divine voice rather than human. It was there, in the middle of that feast and that blasphemy, that Herod became ill and suffered a ghastly death.

Judge: Today's text tells us about the death of Herod. According to the author, that death was God's action, just as Peter's liberation was God's action. The manner in which the two stories are juxtaposed would seem to indicate that Luke also tells us that these are two aspects of the same reality: God intervenes in history. What this passage affirms is what had been affirmed by the prophets and teachers of the Old Testament for a long time: God is not absent from political issues and does not simply let politicians run wild. God opposes injustice and tyranny.

However, one must remember that in the case of tyrants something similar happens to what we saw in the case of those who are God's faithful followers, such as James and Peter. Just as some by faith are able to avoid the sword and others through the same faith die by the sword, it is also true that sometimes God punishes and overthrows tyrants and oppressors and at other times not. But in spite of that, it is still true that "the LORD watches over the way of the righteous, but the way of the wicked will perish" (Psalm 1:6).

Just as the Lord calls us to obedience, be it by freeing us from the sword or by turning us over to the power of the sword, so does the Lord call us to obedience in the middle of the political and other struggles of our days, and in such cases success or the lack thereof is not a final measure or indication of our obedience.

Act: Ask God to give you wisdom and faith to participate in the social and political life of your neighborhood with strength and energy, but without allowing yourself to be carried away by fanaticism. Write down your prayer. Think about the results you expect or would hope to have. Write them down. In a few weeks, come back to this point and read what you wrote.

Sixth Day: Read Acts 12:25–13:3.

See: Here five leaders of the church in Antioch are called "prophets and teachers." It is not clear whether these are two different titles, meaning that some of the named were "prophets" and the others were "teachers," or whether both words were applied to all of them. In that list, two are well known to the readers of the New Testament: Barnabas and Saul. The fact that Simeon was called "Niger" (meaning "black") would seem to indicate that he was of African descent. Since immediately after that Lucius of Cyrene is mentioned, and Cyrene is a city in North Africa, it has been suggested that Simeon also was from that city, and that he was the Simon of Cyrene who carried the cross of Jesus. It has also been suggested that Manaen, here mentioned as a member of the court of Herod, was the source from which the author of Acts derived much of what he says about Herod.

In any case, note that according to the text the Holy Spirit said to those gathered, "Set apart for me Barnabas and Saul." Paul's missionary calling (as well as Barnabas's) does not come to him privately, but rather the Spirit lets the entire group know that there is a special task for these two. Furthermore, the communal dimension of the calling of Barnabas and Saul is reinforced in that they "laid their hands on them." Barnabas and Saul are called by the Spirit, but it is their faith community that hears and ratifies that call.

Judge: Quite commonly in our churches there is the notion that a call from God is something that one receives privately and individually. If the church does not then acknowledge such a calling, the person who claims it simply says that the church is refusing to acknowledge what the Spirit has said. Here, however, we see the Spirit acting through the community. The Spirit speaks to the group about what Barnabas and Saul are to do.

Could it be that we have not given enough importance to the role of the community of faith in the work of the Spirit, calling each member to his or her own form of ministry?

Do you think that your own faith community can help you discern your own gifts, and what the Spirit is calling you to do or to be?

Act: Make a twofold decision:

First, pray about other members of your community, asking God to help you discern some of their gifts. When you believe you have discerned a particular gift in someone else, tell both that person and other people in your church.

Second, ask others to help you discern your own gifts and calling. God has a task for you. The church should help you discover it.

Seventh Day: Read Acts 13:4-12.

See: The passage deals with the beginning of the first missionary journey of Barnabas and Saul. It is in verse 9 that we are told that Saul was "also known as Paul." This is the first time he is called Paul in the book of Acts. At that point every Roman male had, besides his own name and that of his clan, a family name (somewhat like today we have "last names"). "Paul" was the Roman family name, or the last name, of the apostle. Also, it was customary for parents to give children a particular name by which they were known to their friends and family. Quite often, that name was taken from the cultural tradition from which the family stemmed. In this case, "Saul" was the name of the only king of Israel who belonged to the tribe of Benjamin, which was also the tribe of Paul and his family. Therefore, "Saul" seems to have been something like his familiar name, used particularly among Jews.

That is why the author of Acts calls him "Saul" in the beginning of the book, where he is mostly among Jews, but when the mission to the Gentiles begins he is called "Paul."

Judge: It is often said that "Paul" was a name that Saul took as a result of his conversion, and it points to the radical change that took place in him. This is not true. Actually, Acts continues calling him "Saul" until the very beginning of the mission to the Gentiles. What is true is that Saul/Paul is a bridge personality, and that this function is made manifest in his duality of names. He was a Jew, as he himself strongly affirmed in Philippians 3:5. But he was also a Roman citizen, and an able speaker and writer in Greek. As a Jew, although at first he persecuted the church, he was able to understand the message of Jesus and of the reign of God, all of which was the culmination of the hope of Israel (as he himself says in Acts 28:20, it was "for the sake of the hope of Israel" that he did what he did).

However, as a Jew who had spent a significant part of his life away from Palestine, as a Roman citizen who had been educated in Hellenistic culture, he could also interpret that message to the Gentiles in a way Peter and the other apostles could not. It was precisely because he was a bridge personality that Paul could be at the vanguard of the church's mission and open the way toward the future.

"Saul, also known as Paul" reminds us of the situation of many members in our church, for the United States is a land where people of many cultures meet. It is particularly true of people of Hispanic or Latino background, for the United States is actually the fourth largest Spanish-speaking nation in the Americas. There are therefore many people who have a duality of names. A boy who was called "Jesús" by his parents is told by a teacher he cannot have such a name, and is thereafter called "Jesse." People from Latin America, as from other nations, often find it necessary to shorten their names for the sake of convenience. However, these examples point to a much larger reality: There are in our churches and denominations many people who do not belong to the majority culture and who therefore are often marginalized. But the church ought to be aware that when it marginalizes such people it is wasting a significant asset for mission.

People who live in two cultures live in a difficult situation. Frequently there are identity crises and generational conflicts. Still, precisely because they live in two cultures, they serve as a bridge between them. In the case of Hispanics in our churches in the United States, perhaps they could serve as a bridge between the two main cultures in the Western Hemisphere and thus open the way to the future of the church.

Cultures are alive because they are in constant dialogue, conflict, and renewal. Cultures that do not change will necessarily disappear. Therefore, the attempt to "preserve" a culture in all its purity eventually leads to its fossilization and its disappearance. Furthermore, what is true of cultures is also true, to an even greater degree, of the church. The church, incarnate in human reality, must also be incarnate in cultures and in the dialogue and encounters between cultures. The church is not there to defend "pure" cultures, as it is also not there to defend "pure" races.

One of the aspects of the mission of the church is precisely to be part of that dialogue and that movement among cultures. When the church does this, it finds it easier to carry the gospel across cultural boundaries. Therefore, those people in our churches who represent cultures other than the dominant one may well be an instrument by which God is calling the church to its own future.

"Saul, also known as Paul" lived at the same time in several realities. He was a Jew, a Hellenistic Jew, and a Roman citizen. The church always lives in several realities. It certainly is a guardian of the faith given to the apostles, but it must also live out that faith in today's world, with problems and challenges that are quite different from those faced by the early Christians. In our desire to make everything clear and simple, sometimes we think that the multiplicity of realities in which we live is a burden; but the truth is that, much as in the case of "Saul, also known as Paul," it is an opportunity for mission and for obedience to the gospel.

Act: Think about yourself, your church, and your culture.

Do you belong to the dominant culture in the nation? In the community? In your local church?

Do you belong to more than one culture?

Are there people around you who belong to a different culture? How do you relate to them? Are they part of your faith community?

Now ask: What does all this mean for my own vocation as a Christian, and for the life of my local church? Write down your reflection.

For Group Study

Ask the group to consider to what point your church is a bridge linking more than one culture, as Saul/Paul was a bridge. This can be done through several exercises:

One may be simply to look at the members of your church and see who is represented in it. Compare that composition of the church with the composition of your community. If there is a difference, to what is it due?

Make a list of all the hymns that have been sung in your church during the last few weeks. Take into account not only congregational singing, but also special music, anthems, and so forth. Try to determine what culture or cultures they reflect. Compare this with the culture or cultures reflected in the radio or television programming in your own neighborhood.

Now lead the group in a reflection on "Saul, also known as Paul" and what this means for matters of identity. Do we have identity crises in our church, or among us? What are the various cultures, commitments, or functions that seem to be leading us in different directions? Can any of these tensions be bridled in order to contribute to the mission of the church?

SIX

First Day: Read Acts 13:13-52.

See: The Antioch mentioned here must be distinguished from the city from where Paul and Barnabas were coming. This is Antioch of Pisidia in what today is Turkey, not Antioch of Syria whence they came. Upon arriving at a new town, Paul and his companions began their work in the synagogue. This was to be expected, for what they were proclaiming was the fulfillment of the ancient promises made to Israel. Now, in Antioch of Pisidia, Paul and Barnabas went to the synagogue on a Sabbath. After the reading of the Law and the Prophets, they were invited to speak. Paul stood, requested silence, and began his sermon. The first part of the sermon was a summary of the history of Israel, its election, the exodus from Egypt, and so on up to David. Then Paul announced the center of his message, and the surprising point: that the promise has been fulfilled, or "God has brought to Israel a Savior, Jesus, as he promised."

Paul applied all that he said to his audience: "To us the message of this salvation has been sent." The inhabitants of Jerusalem rejected the One who had been sent and turned him over to Pilate to be crucified. Since they had rejected that word of salvation, people in Antioch of Pisidia had the opportunity to respond positively.

But the story did not end there. The Jews of the city, who first rejoiced in hearing that this message was for them, were filled with jealousy when they saw that it was also for the entire town. Their jealousy—their unwillingness to share—made them lose what had been offered. Therefore, what Paul had said about the people in Jerusalem now also became true for these people in Antioch. They too rejected the word of salvation.

Judge: Do not imagine that attitudes such as those described in the text existed only among ancient Jews or among disbelievers. There is a very real danger that they may exist also among us. Therefore, when we hear the message, two things are demanded of us: to receive the message because it is for us, and to share it because it is also for others. The Jews in Antioch of Pisidia wanted to claim the message and keep it for themselves, and therefore they lost it. If we claim the message as if it were ours, and seek to preserve it only for ourselves, we shall likewise lose it. It is quite easy to think that it is only other people who take such an attitude. We, on the other hand, are faithful Christians. We evangelize and share the message. But do we really share it with all, or only with those whose presence will not threaten our own sense of privilege?

The people in the synagogue were quite ready to accept a few converts (what the text calls "devout converts"), but not the entire city. And what about us? When we say that we should evangelize, are we really talking about bringing into the church everyone around us, including those whom society regards with contempt, those who are not well dressed, those whose odor is offensive? Or are we more concerned about making certain that our church is "respectable"? In the biblical text Paul speaks of the power of the message. We also claim that the message is powerful, and rejoice in that. But let us remember that, if we are not faithful to the message of the gospel, if we do not share it with others, that power will turn against us. The gospel will break out of our narrow molds and go elsewhere. And if, on the contrary, we decide to share the message, its power will be with us and we shall be surprised by God's wondrous acts.

Act: Try to share the message with at least one person with whom you have not shared it before. Write down that decision and fold the corner of the page, so that it is quite easy to find again, and do not unbend the page until you have fulfilled that decision.

Second Day: Read Acts 14:1-7.

See: Note that once again the missionaries began their work at the synagogue, and "a great number of both Jews and Greeks became believers." These "Greeks" were not necessarily people from Greece, for that was the name commonly given among Jews to those who, being Gentiles, spoke the common language of the region, Greek. In other words, it was practically synonymous with "Gentiles."

Christian preaching then caused division in the synagogue, and the group that opposed the new doctrine incited the Gentiles who had not believed to oppose the new preachers. This is a pattern that will appear repeatedly in Acts.

"So they remained for a long time." This is quite a surprise in this story. We have just been told that there was strong opposition. What one would expect is that therefore they would decide to go elsewhere. But what they did was exactly the opposite: They remained there for some time. Finally, opposition grew to such a point that there was a plan to kill the missionaries, and it was only then that they decided to go preach elsewhere.

Judge: When we read what happened in Iconium, as well as the entire story of this missionary journey by Barnabas and Paul, the most significant impression that we receive, and one that remains stamped in the memory, is that Barnabas and Paul suffered greatly for the gospel and that in spite of that they were not discouraged nor did they allow fear to rule them. Repeatedly, almost everywhere they arrived, there was a strong current of opposition that frequently led to violence or at least to the missionaries being expelled from the city.

It is important for us to remember this. The gospel that has come to us has been very costly. It cost first of all the crucifixion of Jesus. But it has also cost sacrifice, pain, and even death for countless witnesses. Since most of us are Gentile in origin, we are heirs to the missionary work of Paul and of others who like him went to preach among the Gentiles. Therefore, all these trials and sufferings of Paul and others about which we read here are part of the price paid so that we could have the gospel. The same is true of countless generations through whom the gospel has eventually reached us.

If such is the price that has been paid, are we not obliged to respond by being faithful and by taking up the torch and taking the message to others who have not yet received it?

But above all, each of us should ask: What price have I paid for the gospel? What price am I willing to pay for it, being faithful to it, and taking it to others?

Act: Think of someone you know who has paid a high price for the gospel. Write down that person's name and what you know about him or her. If the person is still living, and if it is at all possible, decide to speak with that person in order to receive advice and inspiration. If it is someone about whom you have read or heard, decide to learn more.

Remember the page in your journal whose corner you folded yesterday. Is it still folded? Why? Could it be that you were not ready to pay the necessary price in speaking to another person? Write down your reflections.

Third Day: Read Acts 14:8-20.

See: As in the case of Antioch in Pisidia, again the passage begins with promising signs. The healing of a lame man gives the missionaries considerable prestige. One could suppose that, since they did not understand the Lycaonian language, all that the missionaries could see was how much people admired them and how attentively they were listening. The text does not tell us what Barnabas and Paul thought, but if it had been us today we would probably have written a glowing letter to those who had sent us, telling them that the entire city was about to be converted. But it was all based on a misunderstanding. The people in the town actually thought that Barnabas and Paul were two gods and were preparing to offer them sacrifice.

(The priests brought oxen to be sacrificed, and the garlands probably were to adorn them before they were sacrificed or to place around the necks of the "gods.")

Finally, Paul and Barnabas realized what was happening. Although they were still quite popular, they saw that the situation was not as promising as they had thought. The respect and attention that the people in Lystra showed was not because they were about to accept the gospel, but rather because they had taken the missionaries for gods. At that point, Barnabas and Paul sought to correct the misunderstanding, even though this meant their prestige would certainly be diminished.

When they finally convinced the people that they were not gods, some of their enemies from other places arrived and they had no difficulty in persuading the multitude to stone Paul and expel him from the city.

Judge: There is much to learn from all this. It is easy for the church to be popular. All it has to do is to say what people want it to say, and to act as people want it to act. Quite often Christians have allowed themselves to think that if we manage to become more popular this will cause the gospel to prosper. We then convince ourselves not to say anything that people will not like, so that the gospel will not suffer.

Many examples of this can be found in the history of the church. In the twentieth century there was a very clear, sad case of this when much of the German church supported the Nazi government and its policies. Many church leaders thought that the Nazi movement was so strong and popular in Germany that to oppose it would mean that the church would lose many members and prestige. Fortunately, there were other Christians who saw things otherwise. They protested against the attitude of the church at large and organized what came to be called the confessing church. Now we know that thanks to that confessing church millions of Jews and Gentiles were saved from the furnaces of Auschwitz and elsewhere. We also know that without that confessing church the witness of Christians in Germany would have been exceedingly shameful.

Similar temptations are still present with us, although not quite as starkly. The temptation is to convince ourselves that the best way to support the gospel is to make it popular, when in truth the only way is the way of obedience. The text we are studying reminds us that the measure of our discipleship is not in the success it achieves or in its popularity, but in its faithfulness. Paul and Barnabas could have "converted" the entire city by simply making a few concessions to idolatry; but such conversion would have been to another gospel, not to the gospel of Jesus Christ.

Today we frequently see very successful preachers who have many followers because they preach a gospel that is easy, and therefore false. The gospel is indeed the good news that in Jesus Christ we are forgiven. But the Lord does not promise that by believing in him all our problems will be solved. On the contrary, what the Lord promised his disciples was they would drink from the bitter cup from which he drank; and he invited them and us to take up his cross and follow him.

Act: Decide to develop a critical attitude toward the various presentations of the "gospel" that you hear and see. If you have the opportunity, try to watch on TV the preaching of a famous evangelist. Listen carefully, asking how much of what is being said is faithful to the gospel of the Crucified, and how much is a way of seeking popularity and success. During the coming weeks, ask the same questions about yourself, about your church, and about the way you hear and live out the gospel.

Fourth Day: Read Acts 14:21-23.

See: This is a very brief passage, but it summarizes a long journey that may well have taken as long as the rest of the entire trip. (Look up on a map of the journeys of Paul the names of these cities, so as to have a clear idea of the journey itself.)

What is most surprising in this brief passage is that Paul and Barnabas return to the same places from which they had earlier had to flee, and where Paul himself had been stoned and left for dead. Once again we are surprised by the zeal of these two preachers. One would have expected them to find a way to return home without visiting again those dangerous places. But they did exactly the opposite, returning precisely by the towns where their own lives had been in danger.

And what is even more remarkable is that in those places, from which they had had to flee, they find communities of Christians whom they comfort, confirm in the faith, and organize by naming "elders" to lead them.

Judge: Do you think that these two missionaries are to be admired because of their willingness to return to places where they still possibly had enemies, and where they would certainly face new difficulties and sufferings?

Do you think that they did this simply because they were stubborn, so as not to appear to give up? Or can you think of other reasons?

Since we are told there were already believers in those cities, ask yourself: Were Paul and Barnabas really free to return home by another way, ignoring those believers? Or were they impelled to visit those cities again because of a solidarity similar to that which we saw in the early chapters, in the church in Jerusalem?

Paul and Barnabas showed that they were faithful followers of Jesus by being faithful to his followers. In those cities there were not only enemies, but also people who had believed. Had they not returned, Paul and Barnabas would have been unfaithful not only to the disciples there, but also to Jesus himself.

Therefore, ask yourself: Are we faithful to one another? Am I faithful to the church, not only by attending regularly and contributing to its budget, but also by being faithful to other members?

Act: Think about a member of your church who may be going through a particularly difficult time. It can be an economic situation, a matter of health, or a spiritual crisis.

Ask yourself: What can I do for that person, in order to show faithfulness?

Write down your answer. Go and do it!

Fifth Day: Read Acts 14:24-28.

See: Here we are told of the return to Antioch. Note that they called the church together and presented a report. Note also that they did not go to Antioch only to give a report and leave immediately, but rather "stayed there with the disciples for some time." Although Paul and Barnabas had been called to be missionaries, this did not mean that they went from one place to another, forgetting what they had left behind. On the contrary, in Acts we see them repeatedly returning to places where they had worked before, in order to strengthen the believers in those places. The same may be seen in Paul's Epistles, by which he continued his ministry in various places that he had visited before.

Judge: The missionaries did not leave Antioch in order never to return. On the contrary, their task would not be complete until they returned and rendered a report to those who sent them. This was not purely a matter of administration, simply giving a report of what had been accomplished. It was certainly that, but it was also much more. It was the matter of the Christian mission always being a two-way street. In mission, both those who send and those who receive benefit. Both receive something. We already saw this in the case of Cornelius, whose conversion was a lesson for Peter as well as for the entire church in Jerusalem. That is also what we see here. The mission that the church of Antioch had sent could be of benefit to new believers in Iconium, Derbe, and Lystra. But it would also be of benefit to the church in Antioch, which would experience something of the power of the gospel in the reports of the missionaries.

That is why in the course of these weeks of study of Acts we have repeatedly seen that when we share the message we benefit too. When we speak of the Lord to others, the Lord himself speaks to us. Have you ever had that experience? If you have witnessed to Jesus Christ and through your witness someone has been converted, most probably you have indeed had such an experience. Your faith has been enriched in the very act of witnessing and seeing the effect of the gospel on someone else. Furthermore, what is true of us as individuals is also true of the church: It is when it carries forth its mission, when it gives much of itself, that the church is most enriched and strengthened.

The mission therefore is not only from the church in Antioch, but also to that same church. Likewise, our witness is not only for others, but also for ourselves and for our own benefit in the development of our faith.

Act: Think about someone whom you have brought to Jesus Christ or someone who has recently joined the church. But rather than thinking of the benefits that such a person has received, as we usually do, think about what you or the church have learned and received from that person. Write it down. Give thanks to God for that person. Make a resolution to approach someone else who is disconnected from the church, not only to invite that person to join your community of faith, but also to receive what the Lord may give you through that person.

Sixth Day: Read Acts 15:1-3.

See: The story that is told here took place some time after the return of Paul and Barnabas to Antioch. The author seems to imply that those who came from Judea were not sent by the church in Jerusalem but rather came on their own. At any rate, what they taught was that in order to be saved, one had to follow the law of Moses, summarized here by the act of circumcision.

As was to be expected, they soon were opposed by Barnabas and Paul, whose ministry had consisted precisely in preaching to the Gentiles and offering them salvation in Christ. Also, as we saw before, this was already the practice of believers in Antioch even before the arrival of Barnabas.

Since apparently those who came from Judea claimed that they represented the directives of the church in Jerusalem, it was decided to send Paul and Barnabas to Jerusalem so that the matter could be discussed and decided.

Judge: There is a deeply rooted human tendency to deny the fundamental principle of the gospel, which is the unmerited grace by which we are saved. What happened in New Testament times has repeatedly happened throughout the history of the Christian church. Some people have taught that in order to be saved one has to abstain from certain foods. Others have taught that one has to have recourse to the sacrament of penance, and thus to pay or atone for sins committed after baptism. Others insist that in order to be saved one has to believe all sorts of doctrinal details. Still others are convinced that people who do not dress as they say will go directly to perdition.

Therefore, the question that was posed in the early church is still with us. Too often we doubt grace, as if it were insufficient. The only thing that the Lord requires of us is for us to believe and to accept. But this seems too easy for us, and then we set out to create other requirements on our own.

There is also the pastor who seems to think that if he kills himself by overwork he will go directly to heaven. Or another pastor who seems to think that if she does not make one more call, God will no longer love her. There are laypeople who work as if their salvation depended on their never having rested.

But if we truly trust in God's grace, it is no longer necessary to justify ourselves, and now we can work and rest knowing that God saves us when we work, and also when we rest.

Act: No matter how strange this may seem, sometimes the most difficult action is to do nothing. Even though throughout this study there have been repeated calls to act, it would be good for you today to stop and, without any action, simply meditate about this unmerited gift of God's grace. Throughout the day, every time you have the opportunity, pray briefly thanking God for such undeserved love. Do not try to earn that love. You already have it. Simply rejoice and enjoy it.

Seventh Day: Read Acts 15:4-29.

See: This is what is usually called "the Council of Jerusalem." Upon arriving at Jerusalem, the delegation from Antioch is well received, except by some among the Pharisees who have joined the church. In first-century Judaism, it was the Pharisees who most insisted on the law as the center of their faith, whereas the Sadducees were more interested in the Temple and its rituals. The Pharisees believed in the final resurrection of the faithful, and the Sadducees did not. Therefore, the Pharisees were closer to the Christians than were the Sadducees, and apparently a good number of Pharisees accepted Jesus as the Messiah. Paul was one of them. Since their tradition so emphasized the law, some among the Pharisees who converted to Christianity still insisted on the need to obey the law, especially on the matter of circumcision.

In order to understand Peter's intervention in the debate, one must remember what we have already studied regarding his vision in Joppa and his experience at the home of Cornelius. When dealing with the debate arising out of the practices and the mission of the church in Antioch, Peter went back to that experience. It is on the basis of it that he affirmed that salvation through God's grace is offered to Jews as well as to Gentiles, and that this is true without having to impose on Gentiles the "yoke" of the law. Once Peter reminded them of the Cornelius episode, apparently they were all satisfied and ready to listen to what God had done among the Gentiles through Barnabas and Paul.

Judge: There are many different people in the church. Some of us belong to Spanish-speaking congregations that are part of denominations in which English is most common. Others are Korean speaking. Some of us worship in congregations in which more than one language is spoken. Many worship in congregations where there are people from different countries of origin. Even within our own local congregations there are differences. We have people belonging to different generations. Some people want to continue doing things as they were done before, while others wish to experiment with new ways of doing the same things. Some of our congregations—although not enough of them—include people from different walks of life, different levels of income, and different levels of education.

All these differences can certainly cause difficulties. Some wish to sing a certain type of music, and others prefer another. Some believe that the service should be formal and even austere, while others believe that the service should be more spontaneous, allowing freedom for all present to say what they wish. Some people believe that it is time to transfer positions of responsibility to a younger generation, while others insist on the value of experience.

Even though such problems tend to discourage us, we must begin by acknowledging that if we did not have such problems, that very fact would be a sign of an even greater evil. If all the members of a church belong to the same generation, the same social class, the same country of origin, and the same theological persuasion, that probably means that the evangelizing and missionary spirit has disappeared. The church will be little more than a social club for people who are "like us."

Therefore, differences within the church, no matter how painful they may seem, are a sign of vitality. A church in which everybody is alike and everybody thinks the same is probably either a dead church or one about to die. Consider what would have happened if the early church had never faced the matter of the admission of Gentiles. Differences are an indication that we are still evangelizing and bringing in people who are different from ourselves.

On the other hand, it is important to prevent differences from becoming divisive. How can this be managed? Perhaps the text gives us some guidance. What is decided in that meeting in Jerusalem is that the Gentiles will not be subjected to the laws of the Jews, except in that minimum that will be necessary in order to fulfill the moral principles of the law and to keep communion with Jewish Christians. Gentiles do not have to become Jews. Nor do Jews have to become Gentiles. What they all have to do is to leave aside their exclusivism in order to accept the differences that exist among them.

Act: In your notebook, write down your answers to the following questions:

What are the main differences in my church (or in my Bible study group)? Are we so uniform that those who are different will not feel welcome?

Do we know how to rejoice in our diversity? How do we show it?

Is there any danger that our diversity might become division? If so, what must we do in order to avoid that danger?

Share your reflections with others.

For Group Study

Ask the group to play-act the passage. Some should be the Christian Pharisees from Jerusalem. Others Paul, Barnabas, Peter, and the others who gathered to discuss the subject of the acceptance of Gentiles. Assign the main roles beforehand, so that people may prepare for them. In the group meeting, after reading the passage, ask those who have prepared to do so to act out the discussion that took place in Jerusalem.

Then lead the group in a discussion of whether there are any parallels between that passage and our present situation.

W E E K
SEVEN

First Day: Read Acts 15:30-35.

See: The passage does not require much explanation. As had been agreed, Judas Barsabbas and Silas go to Antioch. The phrase "they were sent off" in verse 30 may refer not only to these two, but also to those who had earlier come from Antioch to Jerusalem, including Barnabas and Paul.

They were received joyfully but formally. The word that the NRSV translates as "delivered" was then employed for the formal presentation of a letter or other document. The letter itself was read to the congregation, and this resulted in their rejoicing, apparently because the Gentile Christians in Antioch were worried about the possibility that those in Jerusalem would tell them that they would have to be circumcised and obey the law, and worried also over the possible breach this would create.

As the prophets they were, Judas and Silas preached in the congregation, and their preaching resulted in encouragement and strength. The "some time" they remained there could have been a few weeks or even more than a year. The text does not tell us. Then, when they were ready to return to Jerusalem, the church in Antioch gave them a formal farewell.

Judge: Why do you think that the Christians in Antioch rejoiced when they received the letter from Jerusalem? After all, they were free to follow their own path and do as they wished, without having to consult with those in Jerusalem. But unity and love among Christians require that every effort be made to avoid divisions and squabbles and to promote mutual understanding and acceptance. For the church in Antioch, relations with the church in

Jerusalem—and with the many others that Paul, Barnabas, and others had been establishing—was important.

Unfortunately, there are today too many Christians who think that all that is important is their own congregation, or at most their denomination. If in another church there is a different sort of worship, or some slight doctrinal difference, then we are quite ready to ignore or even attack each other. Some churches break away from others because they do not like the pastor or because there are women preachers or because they do not like how communion is celebrated. When people look at the church from outside they see our divisions and squabbles, and therefore they do not believe our witness.

Does your church value its relationships with other congregations and denominations?

Do you accept such people as sisters and brothers in the faith?

Do you make an effort to understand their viewpoints and their Christian experience?

Do you work together with them for a better world?

Act: Make a resolution to approach a brother or sister from another church. Talk to that person, not in order to try to convince him or her to come to your church, but rather to understand his or her perspective and experience of faith.

Visit another church, not to join it or to seek members for your own church, but simply to worship with this other part of the household of God. Invite someone from that other church to visit yours, making it clear that you are not inviting them to join your church, but simply to know it and the people who worship with you. Write down the results.

Second Day: Read Acts 15:36-41.

See: On reading Acts, many receive the impression that Paul spent his time running from one place to another, always preaching the gospel in new places. The reason for this is that, as we have seen repeatedly, Acts summarizes in a few lines what may well have taken months or even years. According to the text we are studying today, Paul's purpose in this second journey was to "return and visit the believers in every city where we proclaimed the word of the Lord and see how they are doing." Even though the Spirit will carry that mission further, and lead the missionaries to new lands, that happens only after they have visited those churches founded earlier. Therefore, in very few verses the author takes us back through what is almost the entire itinerary that Paul and Barnabas followed in their earlier journey.

Judge: This is important, because frequently in our churches a poor reading of Acts has led to a flawed missionary strategy. That faulty reading convinces us that what the Spirit wished Paul to do, and also wishes us to do, is simply to go from one place to another preaching and founding churches. The result has been a vast number of churches in which people who have been recently converted, with practically no knowledge of Scripture or the implications of faith in these complex times, lack the necessary help and guidance to mature in their faith. Also as a result of the same reading of Acts, in some circles it appears that the calling of an evangelist is higher than the calling of a pastor.

Thus, people speak of how many churches they have founded and especially of how many people were converted, but much less is said about the much more difficult task of nourishing, comforting, and challenging all those new believers in new churches. We thus forget that Paul, besides sometimes spending more than a year in a town, returned to the same places as often as possible, and that his letters, which are so helpful to us today, are a result of his pastoral interest—the same interest that led him to suggest to Barnabas a new journey in order to visit people in the churches they had founded, and "see how they are doing."

The result of such a faulty reading of Acts has often been tragic. Some people who have recently been converted find themselves being carried away "by every wind of doctrine" (Ephesians 4:14) because they have not been led to the maturity they need to enable them to discern true from false teaching. Anyone who comes to them with a new and even far-fetched interpretation of Scripture leads them astray. Others have memorized what they were taught, and, although they do not allow themselves to be carried by every wind of doctrine, they certainly have not reached the maturity necessary to face the unexpected challenges of each new day.

We need, besides evangelists and missionaries, pastors and teachers—women and men who study and preach Scripture in congregations and who with them inquire how we are to respond as faithful believers to the challenges of today.

Act: The very fact that you have been studying the book of Acts for more than six weeks shows that you are interested in careful biblical study. Ask yourself, How can I share what I learn with other people in the church? Could it be that God is calling me to be a teacher or a pastor?

Pray over this. Write down your reflections. Discuss them with your pastor and with other people in your church.

Third Day: Read Acts 16:1-5.

See: Timothy must have been very young, since much later the author of the pastoral letters tells us that when Paul was an old man, Timothy was still relatively young (1 Timothy 4:12; 2 Timothy 2:22). He was the son of a Jewish mother and a pagan ("Greek") father. According to Jewish law, the offspring of a Jewish mother were considered Israelites. Paul wished to take Timothy with him, but he was afraid that Timothy's being an uncircumcised Jew would create serious difficulties with other Jews. The phrase "they all knew that his father was a Greek" implies that his uncircumcised condition was generally known. Therefore, Paul decides to circumcise Timothy. (Compare this with Galatians 2:3, where Titus, whose origin is Gentile, is not circumcised.)

Judge: In Timothy's joining the missionary team we have an important lesson. He was well spoken of, but he was young and had no experience. Although elsewhere we are told that both his mother and grandmother were believers (2 Timothy 1:5; 3:15), it is also true that he had not been raised as a good Jew, and that his youth and lack of experience could have made Paul doubt, especially after the episode of John Mark abandoning him and Barnabas. However, part of Paul's mission consists in recruiting those who will continue and expand the mission. In some of our churches, we are not happy unless we control everything. Those who have held positions of authority for a certain length of time believe that they should retain that authority forever.

Thus, instead of preparing new generations to take over positions of responsibility and allowing them to occupy those positions as soon as they are ready, we wait until there are conflicts in which the more elderly seek to retain control, while the younger members either clash with the previous generation as they seek more responsibility or simply leave the church for other spheres of action where they are better received.

Act: Look around yourself. Are there in your church people who are capable of greater responsibility than they now have? Think about such people one by one. Consider how to invite and challenge them to take such responsibilities. Make certain, the next time that there is an opportunity to suggest names for leadership positions, to bring forward some of those people. Write down their names. Pray for them. Consider what you can do in order to help this younger generation mature in its faith. Write down your reflections.

Fourth Day: Read Acts 16:6-10.

See: The text begins with a vision that Paul had in Troas, where a Macedonian man appeared before him asking him to come and help. This could be a dream or some other sort of vision. The text does not explain it. Macedonia was the region north of Greece whence three centuries before Alexander the Great had launched his great military campaign. Now it was a Roman province.

Since Macedonia was in Europe and Troas was in Asia, in order to reach Macedonia Paul had to cross the sea. Therefore, the result of this vision was that the mission of Paul and his companions went beyond Asia, reaching Europe for the first time.

Judge: Paul was at Troas, practically where the Asian continent ended. He had already gone quite far. He was tired (and there are some indications that he might even have been ill). It was time to return and to declare that he had fulfilled his purpose.

Then comes the vision of the Macedonian man asking for help, and Acts tells us that they immediately began making arrangements to leave for Macedonia. In spite of fatigue, and also in spite of any other plan, the request for help evokes an immediate response. The result is an entire new field of service and a church that soon began to flourish. We know from the letters of Paul that the church in Philippi, which was in Macedonia, was among the most helpful and generous.

When the Lord called Paul on the road to Damascus, the only instruction that Paul received was to continue on to Damascus, where he would be told what to do. When, much later, the Lord called him to his missionary enterprise, there were also very few details as to what he was to do. Thus, Paul's life was a continuing series of calls, each wider than the previous one. Paul was not content with knowing that God had called him years ago to be a believer or that the same God called him later to be a missionary.

It is possible that God is calling you today to a new task, a new ministry, a new adventure. Could that be the case?

Act: Pray: Lord, help me to see what you wish me to do now. Are you calling me to a new adventure of faith?

Continue your prayer for some time. Write down whatever answers you receive. Discuss them with others in your community of faith.

Fifth Day: Read Acts 16:11-15.

See: The missionaries have already been for a few days in Philippi, and they have inquired about the synagogue. The word that the Greek text uses here may refer either to a synagogue or to any other place where people gather for worship. Therefore, what is implied is that they were seeking a synagogue, as they usually did in every new town, and what they actually found was a group of women praying. It could not be a synagogue, for according to the law the synagogue could not gather unless there were at least ten males present.

There is an interesting irony. Paul received the vision of a "man" calling him (verses 9-10). The word that is used there emphasizes his gender. However, what Paul found in Philippi in response to the man's call was a group of women. And the first leader of the newly born church in Europe was a woman, Lydia of Thyatira. Her home provided the nucleus of that new church, and was the center of Paul's missionary activity in Philippi.

Judge: Although he was called to Macedonia by the vision of a man, what Paul found there was a group of women. Can you guess or imagine why that contrast? Could it be perhaps because, if the vision had been of a woman, Paul would have been less inclined to follow it? It is impossible to know. But what is clear in the text is that the vision implies much more than Paul himself could imagine: a group of women, and out of it, the birth of the church in an entire continent.

Christian discipleship requires that we be constantly attentive to voices crying for help and that we respond with genuine interest and support, even while being conscious that sometimes what we are being asked for is not exactly what people require or wish.

Sometimes such voices are explicit and do tell us what is needed. A sick person asks for prayers. An elderly person requests transportation.

But in fact most often those who need something tell us indirectly. A young woman complains that her parents do not let her do what she wishes, but in fact what bothers her is not that but rather that her parents do not seem to pay attention to her problems. While her voice calls for freedom, what she is really asking for is attention. An employee complains of a low salary, when in truth what bothers him is that his low wages seem to be an indication of how little he is appreciated. Thus, although his voice asks for more money, what he really wishes to have is more appreciation and respect. In order to know what we are being asked for, we must listen with great attention.

What is true of individuals is also true of communities. In order to know what they really wish and need, one must listen. Thus, when we decide to serve the community around our church, the first thing we must do is to listen attentively. We have to get to know that community. We have to earn its trust, so that we may be told what are the real problems existing there. And, once we begin our action, we must continue listening in order to make whatever adjustments are necessary.

Act: Think about someone who has requested your help. What were you asked for? Was that really what the person wanted or needed? Write down your reflections. Make it a point, from now on, when someone addresses you, to be alert for those calls or requests that may hide behind what is being said.

Sixth Day: Read Acts 16:16-24.

See: In Macedonia, the missionaries settled in Philippi, the main city in the area. Three important events took place there. The first of these was the conversion of Lydia, about which we have already read.

The second important incident was the healing of a woman with a spirit of divination. At first, Paul paid no attention to what the young woman (or the evil spirit who spoke through her) said; but eventually he did feel the need to respond. Note that what the evil spirit said is true (verse 17). But, even though true, the witness of such a spirit is not a good thing to be welcomed. Eventually, Paul chastised the spirit and ordered it out of the young woman. It was at that point that her owners, upset because Paul had spoiled their business by healing the girl, presented an accusation against Paul and Silas. They accused them not of having healed the young woman, but rather of disturbing the peace. As a result, the missionaries were flogged and imprisoned.

Unlike today, a charge of disturbing the peace was a very serious matter. There were cases in which the Roman Empire punished an entire city, killing thousands of its residents, for disturbing the peace. It certainly was a crime punishable by death, for the Empire was very much concerned about keeping order and avoiding riots or other disturbances that might lead to rebellion.

Judge: There are two important elements in this text. The first is that, although what the evil spirit said was true, Paul did not accept its witness. The witness of this spirit, even though seemingly good and certainly true, was bad.

Unfortunately, too often the church has forgotten this. Repeatedly, because a particular dictator declared himself to be Christian, or simply because he allowed Christian preaching, the church was all too ready to forget about that dictator's crimes and even to praise him in order to gain further support. Sometimes, when Christians have heard a famous person witness to Jesus

Christ, they have turned that person into a sort of hero, even though his or her actions belied the witness itself.

Do you think that the church should accept and listen to such witnesses? Do you know any such cases today? (For instance, famous actors, singers, or athletes whose lives of unbridled luxury belie the gospel and who at the same time claim to be born again; corrupt or insensitive politicians who ignore or oppress the weak, and who court the support of Christians by claiming to be followers of Jesus.)

The second point worthy of notice in this text is that our good actions may well lead us to difficulties. We live in a world full of sin and evil, a world in which many people profit from the suffering of others (like the young woman's owners). In such circumstances, if we oppose that evil and seek to find ways to eliminate it, those who benefit from the existing situation will resent it. They will even find some charge to bring against the church or against Christians, without letting it be known that they are defending their own interests.

That is why much of what the church says and does turns out to be controversial. We might wish for the church to stay out of controversy, but the truth is that good itself is controversial. When the church acts against vice, someone will be disturbed and will find a reason to attack the church. When the church feeds the hungry, there frequently are merchants and others who are disturbed because the church is competing with their business. When the church defends someone who is being exploited, there is always an exploiter who says that the church ought not to meddle in such matters.

The church should neither fear controversy nor seek it. The purpose of the church is not to create controversies. Its purpose is to serve God by preaching the gospel and by serving others. But, on the other hand, if that preaching or that service lead to controversy, that should be neither cause nor excuse to abandon what we are doing.

Act: Think of an occasion (the more recent, the better) in which there was talk in your church of doing something or taking some action, and it was decided not to do so because it could lead to disagreements. Think and pray over the matter, asking yourself whether some good that could have been done was not done, or whether the church failed in its mission. Write down your reflections. Make it a point, the next time someone objects to some particular action or witness as controversial, to make certain that this is not used as an excuse not to act as required by the gospel. Write down your resolution. Share your reflections with someone else in your church.

Seventh Day: Read Acts 16:25-34.

See: The third incident that takes place in Philippi, and the best known, is the conversion of the jailer in that city. In spite of being sore from their floggings, and tied, Paul and Silas sang in the middle of the night. Their fellow prisoners heard their singing—which may be mentioned in the narrative in order to make clear that these prisoners were also witnesses to the miracles that would take place. Suddenly there was an earthquake. What made it clear that this was a miraculous event, not just a natural phenomenon, was that the doors were opened and the chains of the prisoners set loose. However, no one fled. Interestingly, we are not told why. At any rate, the jailer, apparently thinking that the prisoners had fled and that therefore his honor had been destroyed, prepared to kill himself when Paul told him that all the prisoners were still there.

Then came the famous question of the jailer, who at the feet of Paul and Silas asked them, "What must I do to be saved?"

Quite possibly the question itself did not have the theological dimensions lent to it in later preaching. The jailer was afraid because of the earthquake, which was proof of the divine wrath over the manner in which the missionaries had been treated. What he sought was to escape whatever punishment such a powerful God had prepared for him. How could he be saved from such punishment? Verse 31 includes the famous answer of the missionaries: "Believe on the Lord Jesus, and you will be saved, you and your household."

The fact that the author said that this is what both Paul and Silas told the jailer is an indication that this was not a simple formula that the two repeated in unison. It is rather that, responding to the question of the jailer, the missionaries expounded to him the message of the gospel. In response to that message, the jailer washed their wounds and was then baptized, together with all his family.

Judge: The story of the jailer in Philippi is well known. The phrase that is usually emphasized in our preaching is, "Believe on the Lord Jesus, and you will be saved, you and your household." It is proper to underscore that phrase, for it is certainly the high point of the narrative. However, when we look at the entire passage, we see some other dimensions of this conversion that are often overlooked.

Most remarkable is the change that took place in the jailer himself when he was converted. This was a man whose career and concern for professional prestige were such that, when he thought that his prisoners had escaped, he was ready to kill himself. For him life was worthless without that prestige and respect. Now, after his conversion, he took these two prisoners, who had been entrusted to him with so much insistence, out of prison, washed their wounds, and took them to his house to eat. Apparently, his career and professional prestige were no longer as important as they had been before, to the point that he was willing to risk them by caring for Paul and Silas and offering them hospitality.

Such is the nature of true conversion. Today we often speak of a "conversion" that has no teeth. On the basis of this text, we often claim that "to be saved, all you have to do is believe in Jesus Christ." What we do not say, and often do not even see, is that belief in Jesus Christ involves much more than mere assent. It is also a radical change, not only in the manner in which we live, but even in the values whereby we measure success in life. For the rich person who used to think that money was everything, conversion must include a new life in which *all* economic resources are at God's disposal. For the professional who thought that success in life was in prestige and in the respect of others, conversion must lead to seeking ways in which that very profession may turn out to be of service to others—particularly to those most in need of service. And, if such means cannot be found, then conversion may well mean seeking a new occupation or means of service.

The gospel includes the good news that our lives can be useful in God's reign. It also includes the good news that the value of our life does not depend on how society at large assesses it. For the jailer in Philippi, life no longer had to be measured on the basis of whether or not he fulfilled his task of holding his prisoners. For us, if we have truly received the gospel, the good news includes freedom to be obedient, to be authentic, in spite of all the social pressure in other directions.

Act: Ask yourself: What aspects of your life have not yet been reached by a radical conversion? Your dreams? Your business? Your family life? Your relationships with other people?

Write down your reflections by way of confession. Then pray, placing all of this in God's hands and asking God to grant you a new heart and a new life.

For Group Study

Review the various points studied during these days regarding the vision of the Macedonian man and the work of Paul in Philippi. The vision led Paul to undertake a new mission. What new visions must our church have regarding its mission? To what new venture may the Lord be calling us today?

Paul expected a man and found a group of women. Ask: Have we ever had experiences when something was asked of us when in truth something else was needed? Remember that when help is requested of us, and even when we are asked for something that we should not grant (for instance, when an alcoholic asks for a drink), below that request there is quite frequently a deeper need to which we can indeed respond. The deepest need of all is the need for the gospel, the need for communion with God, the need for life to have meaning.

Paul did not accept the witness of the evil spirit, even though what it said was true. Should we be ready to accept any witness from anybody or any institution, simply because it proclaims Jesus, no matter who is giving the witness itself?

Paul's good deed led to his imprisonment and flogging. Are we ready to be faithful and to do what is right, even though this could lead to rejection and even to suffering? Can the group think of some such case today?

The jailer's conversion was radical. What aspects of our life are most difficult for us to turn over to the Lord? How can we support one another in order to overcome that difficulty?

W E E K
EIGHT

First Day: Read Acts 16:35-40.

See: The day after the earthquake, the authorities decided to free Paul and Silas. We are not told why they reached such a decision. One can imagine that they knew, or at least suspected, that the charges against Paul and Silas were false. Perhaps they had agreed to arrest and flog them simply in order to satisfy the demands of a populace that threatened to riot. Now that the atmosphere was calmer, the magistrates would deem it best simply to let the prisoners go free and invite them to leave without further ado.

But Paul surprised them by letting them know that both he and Silas were Roman citizens. In order to understand the significance of this, it is important to know that not all inhabitants of the Roman Empire were considered citizens. Only a few enjoyed such a title and the privileges it implied. In Rome itself, not all were citizens and even fewer in the more distant areas of the Empire. Therefore, the magistrates did not even imagine that these two preachers of a strange doctrine could be Roman citizens.

To complicate matters further, there was a very ancient law declaring that one of the privileges of Roman citizenship was that a citizen could not be punished by flogging. Anyone disobeying such a law would suffer all the weight of Roman authority. But that is precisely what had been done with Paul and Silas: they had been flogged publicly and even without any sort of trial. Now it was the magistrates who were worried. They begged Paul and Silas to leave the city without creating any greater difficulties. But Paul and Silas refused to do so. Rather, they left the jail, went to Lydia's home (that is, they felt free to move around the city), they exhorted the church. Only then did they go elsewhere.

Judge: The magistrates at Philippi were victims of their own prejudices. They did not even imagine that these strange Jewish preachers could be Roman citizens. The same thing happens quite often all around us in the United States. The police arrest a Latino or Latina and, without any further question, they decide that the person is poor, ignorant, lacking in resources or support, and probably also lacking legal documents. On the basis of such prejudices, they feel free to mistreat the person arrested. Then they discover their mistake, either because someone decides to defend that person, or because they made a mistake and the person arrested was not exactly what they thought. Now it is they, who were supposed to be guardians of the law, who are found to have broken it. They are victims of their own prejudice.

On the other hand, if we belong to a minority it is important for us to remember the example of Paul and Silas. They were beaten and imprisoned illegally. When the authorities came to ask them to leave the city, as if they had to sneak out, they refused to do so. Instead of leaving the city surreptitiously, they made use of their rights and went quite openly to visit Lydia. Likewise, when we find ourselves in situations such as the one just described it is important for us to insist on our rights and our dignity, not just for ourselves, but because denying us justice or dignity is also a crime against all others who look like us, and the law of the land has been broken even by those who were supposed to be its defenders.

Act: Have you ever found yourself harboring prejudices against others by reason of the way they looked, how they spoke, what they said? Have you ever found yourself at the other end of prejudice, being judged unfairly by those who did not really know you? Think about ways in which you should act in such situations. Write down your reflections.

Second Day: Read Acts 17:1-9.

See: Follow the route of Paul and his companions on a map of Paul's journeys. The distance from Philippi to Thessalonica was some thirty miles. Thus the journey would take at least two or three days. The mention of Amphipolis and Apollonia would seem to indicate that they stopped in each of those places.

In Thessalonica, the missionaries have been preaching for at least a little over two weeks ("three sabbath days"), and the results are good. However, some of the Jews who have not believed the message (those who believed were mostly also from the synagogue) are said to have become "jealous." The reference to "ruffians in the marketplaces" depicts a situation well known in our cities. These were people who apparently had nothing better to do than simply hang out in public places. They were at the core of the mob that created an uproar. After failing to find the missionaries, they took hold of Jason, in whose home Paul and Silas were lodging, and took him before the authorities, accusing him of having as guests people who turn "the world upside down," and who act "contrary to the decrees of the emperor, saying that there is another king named Jesus."

Judge: As we move deeper into the story in Acts, we see that the charges against Christians become increasingly serious. At first there were charges among Jews that they somehow subverted the faith of Israel—and those charges remain present throughout the book. Then, in Philippi, the owners of the young woman whom they healed accused the missionaries of teaching and promoting customs that were not lawful for Romans (see 16:21). Now, in Thessalonica, they were accused of being disloyal to the emperor by proclaiming another king.

Such charges were partly false, partly true. They were false inasmuch as they did not reflect the true motives for which the missionaries and Jason were accused. But they were true in that the missionaries were indeed inviting their converts to follow a way of life that was not sanctioned by the Empire, and also because the absolute lordship of Jesus questions the lordship of the emperor, which also claims to be absolute.

There is an undeniable subversive dimension in Christian faith. Those who accused the missionaries correctly said that they were turning the world upside down. An essential part of the Christian faith is the claim that there is a difference between the world as it is and the world as God wishes it to be. The reign of Caesar is not the same as the reign of God. Where God is king, there can be no other absolute ruler. Therefore, every absolutism must be brought down. Neither nationalist absolutism, nor idealist absolutism of the right or the left, nor military absolutism, nor even ecclesiastical absolutism is compatible with Christian faith. If we faithfully preach the message of the gospel, we too will be accused of subverting the creeds and customs of the present world by claiming that there is indeed another king, Jesus.

Unfortunately, it is quite common for people in our churches to believe that it is possible to preach or to believe the gospel of Jesus Christ without that dimension that turns the world upside down, subverts all absolutisms, and questions every present order, judging it not on the basis of preconceived ideologies but on the basis of the coming reign of God. In truth, the full preaching of the gospel must subvert the order, and must subvert even subversion itself. Is that the message we preach and whereby we live?

Act: Think of any particular element or custom in the society or community where you live that the gospel ought to subvert (for instance, the commonly held notion that success in life is the same as economic success). Write a few lines in your notebook describing that situation. Consider what you can and should do in order to subvert it. Write down your reflections.

Third Day: Read Acts 17:10-14.

See: The missionaries, who apparently remained hidden in Thessalonica, left during the night to Beroea, a city that was not on any of the main thoroughfares, and somewhat distant from Thessalonica. There once again they began their teaching in the synagogue. The author tells us that the Jews there were "more receptive" (literally, "better born") than those in Thessalonica, for they were ready to study Scripture and see whether what Paul said was true.

According to verse 12, the success of the mission was remarkable. This is the second time that Acts refers to "Greek women . . . of high standing."

Eventually, the news arrived in Thessalonica of what was happening in Beroea, and the same people who stirred up the population of Thessalonica did the same in Beroea. As a result, Paul had to be sent "immediately" to the coast, while Silas and Timothy (who we had not been told was with them) remained in Beroea.

Judge: One striking element in this story is that the people who began persecuting Paul and his companions in Thessalonica out of jealousy, and who tried to bring false charges against them, now continue their persecution as far as Beroea—which was several days' journey away.

That is what often happens when emotions are stirred up. The charge of subversion presented in Thessalonica, and which has so often been made against the most faithful, even though at first a means to cover other motivations, eventually builds its own impetus, and remains even when the original motivation has been forgotten.

I know of a case in Latin America of a doctor who, embittered because an institution of the church had not dealt fairly with his father many years before, began accusing that institution and all that had anything to do with it of being subversive. This he did even though none of those present in the institution at the time were there when his father was unjustly treated. When he first published his initial charges, he was quite aware that he did this by way of revenge. But as time passed, he became increasingly convinced of the charges that he himself had created, and eventually became the spokesperson for a group that was using his resentment for its own ends. Unfortunately, in such cases, as in the case of the Jews in Thessalonica, dialogue becomes impossible.

What are Christians to do when such things happen? Is the attitude of Paul and his companions an example for us? They simply continued teaching, preaching, and living out what they considered to be the gospel.

Act: Think about someone, or some group in your congregation or in your own denomination, about whom you do not think very highly. Stop to consider the sources and the reasons you hold such a position. Consider the possibility that at least part of your feelings and opinions may be due to prejudice on your part, or on the part of someone who has informed you about that person. If it is at all possible to doubt whatever evil you have heard about that person or group, do so. Ask God to help you abstain from unfounded or inflexible judgments. Write down your reflections.

Fourth Day: Read Acts 17:15-21.

See: Paul was in Athens not in order to preach, but simply to wait for his companions. However, as he waited his reaction to the situation in Athens was typical of that of any good Jew or Christian, for "he was deeply distressed to see that the city was full of idols."

Athens had seen better times. Greece was one of the most impoverished areas of the Roman Empire. The city itself was relatively underpopulated, but it still retained much of its ancient glory. In a city with a declining population, but still boasting splendid temples, it is no surprise that Paul was concerned over such a show of idolatry.

However, Athens' fame was not limited to its temples. Even more famous were its philosophers and its authors. That very active intellectual life had led the Athenians to relish "telling or hearing something new."

Judge: When we read a biblical story, it is normal for us to identify ourselves with the believers or the faithful people in the particular text, and to place ourselves there within the story. Thus, for instance, when we read about the missionary journeys of Paul, our tendency is to place ourselves next to Paul and his companions in order to learn from them. That certainly is good and useful. But it is also helpful now and then to consider the possibility of finding ourselves in the place of those who do not seem to be as good or as admirable.

As we read today's text, let us think about those Athenians who listened, not because they really wished to learn anything, but out of a superficial curiosity, out of a desire to hear something new. That comes very close to what we today call "faddism."

Just as it was in Athens, so also today in many of our churches we go for the latest fad. There are people ready to hear anything from anyone, as long as it is new. "Teachers" arrive with a new and strange interpretation of a particular Bible text, and people follow their teachings, until another one appears that is even stranger. The result of all this is that people are scandalized, the church is divided, and the world does not believe.

Act: First of all, consider the possibility that you too may be inclined to follow the latest fad.

Do you allow yourself to be carried away by every wind of doctrine? Are you impressed by strange and complicated interpretations of the Bible?

In that case, make a decision to be more careful in judging what you hear. Write down some of the fads that impressed you in the past but which you no longer find interesting.

On the other hand, if you are worried over the faddism of some of the members of your church community, think about ways in which you can strengthen them so that they may not be carried away by any whim of doctrine. Write down some of your possible answers or actions.

For instance, you may teach in Sunday school, read a good book and then share with the congregation what you have learned, recommend and make use of good solid reading, and other such things.

Fifth Day: Read Acts 17:22-34.

See: Responding to the curiosity of the philosophers, Paul addressed them in the speech we are now studying. It was a respectful speech, which even made use of what earlier philosophers had said. There are in it several quotations of ancient Greek teachers, and this would show his audience that Paul knew their culture and even respected it. Then Paul began presenting the God he preaches, referring to the works of creation (verses 24-29). Those who heard him could follow his argument and accept what he was saying without any major difficulties, for also among the ancient philosophers the notion existed of a Supreme Being, the source of all that exists.

When we get to verse 30, the entire tone of the speech changes. It is no longer a matter of eternal truths or facts all can corroborate by looking at creation, but of what God has done and is doing. This includes having fixed a time for judgment, and having appointed Jesus Christ.

It was at this point that most of his audience lost interest. Some mocked what Paul had to say, and others excused themselves, telling him that they would listen to him some other time. The speech that began so well was about to end poorly. In spite of this, some did believe. The author gives us the names of two believers, which seems to indicate that they eventually became leaders of the church. But in spite of that, the fact remains that Paul did not have very much success in Athens.

Judge: If Paul had stopped his speech after mentioning the "unknown God" and creation, probably many of those present would have praised his knowledge and his eloquence. At the beginning of his speech, Paul had cultivated the goodwill of his audience by referring to their culture and traditions. On the other hand, by speaking of judgment, Jesus, and resurrection, he seemed to spoil the whole thing. Is that true?

Paul had several alternatives, one of which was to continue his speech along the same lines that he began, saying things that his audience would be quite ready to accept. By so doing, he could have left the Areopagus surrounded by admirers and perhaps even by followers. But had he chosen that route, he would not have been faithful to the message that had been entrusted to him.

Another alternative would have been to tell the Athenians that their culture and traditions were worthless, that they had to abandon all that in order to become Christians. But Paul did not follow that route either.

The route that Paul did follow was different. He told the Athenians that what he was bringing was the message of Jesus Christ, of what God had done in a particular person at a particular time, and about what God demanded of those who were now listening. In other words, Paul did affirm what the Athenians knew on their own, but he still insisted that they needed to accept Jesus Christ and his message.

We often find ourselves in similar circumstances, between two extreme alternatives. On the one hand, there are those who seem to believe that preaching Jesus crucified means rejecting all that human culture and human achievements teach us. In the Areopagus, Paul gave signs of knowing and respecting the culture of the Athenians. Preaching Jesus Christ does not mean to reject whatever our audience is or knows.

On the other hand, there is an easy preaching that tells people what they wish to hear, that makes the gospel a very easy thing, but that in fact does not proclaim the gospel of Jesus Christ.

We live at a time of great general religiosity. Most people we meet believe in something. Most of them even say that they believe in God. But each one wishes to believe in a convenient God, to be shaped after our own fashion and pleasure. Such people are ready to respect Christians, and even say that the church is a good institution. In exchange, sometimes they also expect the church to preach nothing beyond that general religiosity that is part of the surrounding culture, and that does not challenge their faith or their way of life. If we speak only of general moral principles, or of the need to "believe in God" and "serve others," such people will be quite satisfied and will even support and join the church.

But if we tell them that the one that we preach is God made flesh in Jesus Christ and that what we are inviting them to do is not simply to support the church, but to believe in Jesus Christ and follow him, then quite possibly they will leave us, as those who were listening to Paul in the Areopagus also left.

What do you believe should be our attitude in such circumstance? How can we show that attitude?

Act: Pray: "Teach me, Lord, to respect those to whom I speak, to see the value of what they already know and understand. Teach me also to speak to them with courage about the new that you do and the new that you offer in Jesus Christ. In his name I pray. Amen." Think about that prayer, and write down your thoughts.

Sixth Day: Read Acts 18:1-17.

See: Corinth was a flourishing city, the capital of the province of Achaia. Since its wealth was due mostly to its privileged geographical position, which made it a center of trade and transportation, all sorts of people of diverse cultures and walks of life came to it: travelers, merchants, sailors. For a long time, Corinth had been famous for its licentious and disorderly life, to such a point that when people elsewhere were leading an immoral life, it was said that they were "Corinthianizing."

It is significant to point out that this entire passage refers to historical and political events that are known to us through writings that are not part of the New Testament. Such is the case with the edict of Claudius expelling the Jews from Rome, and of the tenure of Gallio, the proconsul of Achaia.

Judge: It has already been stated that the book we are studying, rather than "Acts of the Apostles," should be called "Acts of the Spirit," for the theme of the book is not what the apostles did, but rather what the Spirit does. We have repeatedly seen the action of the Spirit in the community of believers or in the work of Paul and his companions. Here we see another dimension of that action, which is significant for our obedience today: The Spirit also acts in history, sometimes in such a mysterious way that we do not even suspect that action.

There are two examples in this passage. The first is the edict of Claudius expelling the Jews (or at least some of them) from Rome. It is as a result of that edict that Priscilla and Aquila find themselves in Corinth when Paul arrives there. The entire work of that couple, first in Corinth and then in Ephesus, is a result of that edict of a pagan emperor. The second example is the trial before Gallio. Gallio had no intention of protecting Paul. He apparently had little respect either for Paul or for his accusers. But that very contempt on the part of a powerful person gives Paul and other believers the space to carry forth their work.

What is the significance of this for us today? Sometimes we imagine that the Spirit of God is active only in the church, where we see various manifestations of that activity. However, to think that the Spirit acts only in the church is to limit the power and work of the Spirit. Long before Paul reached Corinth the Spirit of God had already prepared the way by leading Priscilla and Aquila to the city. God acts not only in the history of the church and the lives of believers, but also in the history of the world and even in the lives of those who refuse to believe.

Act: Resolve to pay more attention to the news that appears in the press, radio, and television. When reading or hearing such news, consider the possibility that the Spirit of God may be active there. Try to think of some event of a few years ago in which now you can see God's action. Write down your reflection.

Seventh Day: Read Acts 18:18-23.

See: Paul's sojourn in Corinth was prolonged. Quite possibly at that time other churches were founded in nearby towns. In Romans 16:1, Paul speaks of the church in Cenchreae, which was the port of Corinth on the Aegean Sea. And in 2 Corinthians 1:1 he addresses his letter not only to the Corinthians, but also to "all the saints throughout Achaia." At any rate, the time had now come for Paul to return to Antioch, and we are told that he "sailed for Syria." This should be understood to mean that he headed toward Syria and not that he went directly there, for we are then told that he stopped first in Ephesus and then in Caesarea. As the word was then used by the Romans, "Syria" included both what we today call Syria and all of Palestine. After a stop in Ephesus, Paul went on to Caesarea, which was the main port for those traveling to Jerusalem, and then went on to Antioch. At the beginning of that voyage, Priscilla and Aquila accompanied him. They were probably going to Ephesus for business reasons, and Paul, who was lodging with them, took the opportunity to travel with them.

The vow of cutting one's hair was common among Jews at the time. Apparently, some Jews who were traveling would cut their hair and then bring it as a sacrifice to the Temple, in a ceremony signaling purification from the impurity that they might have contracted from Gentiles. In any case, most probably the author mentions this vow that Paul had made in order to underline his continued faithfulness to Jewish religious practices. Paul was not anti-Jewish, nor did he encourage Jews to abandon the practices of their ancestors; but he insisted that those who were not Jews did not have to follow those practices in order to accept Christ and join the church.

From Corinth, Paul went to Ephesus. As you look at his route on a map it seems strange that, in order to go from Corinth to Caesarea, Paul would sail first to Ephesus. This may have been partly due to his desire to accompany Priscilla and Aquila, who were traveling to Ephesus. But it was also the result of the practice of sailing at that time. Sailors always preferred to remain in sight of the shore, or at least to avoid prolonged crossing in the high seas. Therefore, people traveling from Cenchreae toward the east would frequently cross the Aegean toward Ephesus, in order then to continue toward the south and the east. At any rate, from this point on through the rest of the first century Ephesus would become an important city in the history of Christianity. In the book of Acts, Ephesus and its church will occupy the center of the stage until the end of chapter 21.

Finally, Paul returned to Antioch, whence he had departed a long time before.

Judge: Acts does not tell us much about what Paul did in Jerusalem or in Antioch at this time. Furthermore, in the very next verse we shall see him departing on a new journey. However, the very fact that he returned to those two cities provides some important clues regarding the manner in which Paul understood his mission. He had no need to return to either city. He was not like some missionaries today, who have to return periodically to the churches that support their work. Paul supported himself with his own tent-making craft, and he also received a measure of support from the churches he had founded, as is clear in the case of Philippi. When there are economic transactions between Paul and the church in Jerusalem, it is the latter that receives contributions from the Pauline churches, and not vice versa.

Paul's purpose in returning to Jerusalem and Antioch had nothing to do with missionary support, but rather with his own vision of the nature of mission. His mission was not merely to preach the gospel, to gain converts, and to found churches, but included also creating and building up bonds among all Christians and all churches. When someone was converted as a result of Paul's work, Paul joined that person to the church. And when Paul founded a church in Philippi, what he created was not an independent unit, completely isolated from the rest of the body of Christ. That church had its autonomy, and even if one wishes to call it such, its independence; but it could not be the church of Jesus Christ by itself, isolated from the rest of the body.

Today we need something of that understanding of mission. Partly as a reaction to a time when only one church was allowed in a nation or community, we have sometimes gone to the opposite extreme and acted as if the relationship among Christians, and among various Christian communities, were a secondary matter. We say, for instance, that what is important is "believing in Jesus" and that the church is simply a convenient support for that faith, rather than part of the gospel itself. But in the Bible, believing in Jesus implies and requires joining the community of the faithful. Believing in Jesus is a very personal matter, but it is never a private matter.

When we lose that vision, there are several consequences.

The first consequence is that the church becomes something optional for believers. I partake of the life of the church if I feel like it; if I don't, that is acceptable too. After all, what is important is the relationship with the Lord. That is why many of us who are pastors are often told in our visits: "Don't worry, Pastor, I can be a Christian without attending church."

The second consequence is that we limit the function of the church. The church is there to meet *my* spiritual needs. If whatever is being said or done in church on a given day does not respond to those needs, there is no reason for me to participate. Quite often one hears that the church is like a gas station where we receive energy for the rest of the week. That may well be true, but the church is much more than that. The church is part of the gospel; the church is that community which lives out of an expectation of God's reign and in which, therefore, that reign becomes present, no matter how difficult it may be for us to see it. The church is there to respond not only to *my* needs, but to all the needs of all believers, and even of this whole world for which Jesus died.

The third consequence is that some people switch churches as easily as changing a shirt. *I don't like the pastor. That other church is more active. The music over there is better. That one has a better youth program.* We then become like spiritual tourists who seldom have any depth in their knowledge of the places they have visited or the place where they are.

The fourth consequence is that any excuse suffices to divide the church. If, after all, the community of believers is not all that important, any disagreement should suffice for Christians to part company. If a group does not like a particular pastor, they simply go elsewhere to find another one. In some cases, pastors who do not seem to like any particular group simply declare themselves to be independent, become "evangelists," and thus avoid a relationship of long-term commitment with any particular faith community.

Finally, as a consequence of all of this, we end up divided in a multitude of groups that spend more time competing and debating among ourselves than carrying forth the task and being a sign of the work of God's reign in this world.

Over against that vision, there is the one that Acts presents throughout, and which Paul exemplified in this passage. The church is an essential part of Christian life. Its purpose is not only to meet my needs, but to meet the needs of the world, and to be a sign of the work and grace of Jesus Christ.

Act: Reaffirm your commitment to your community of faith. Its members will not always agree on all things, as we can see repeatedly in the book of Acts. But when there are disagreements, make every possible effort to keep the bonds of love and communion. Thus, and only thus, will the world believe. That is why Jesus prayed: "that they may all be one. As you, Father, are in me and I am in you, may they also be in us, so that the world may believe that you have sent me" (John 17:21). Write down your reflections in your notebook. When you are tempted to leave or quarrel with your community of faith, read your own notes once more.

For Group Study

Toward the end of your session, raise some of the following issues:

If your church is involved in some community work jointly with another church, take this opportunity to discuss that work, and how it becomes possible or at least more effective because we work together.

If there is no such common work, ask the group if there is a task in our community that our church should be performing, not alone, but jointly with other churches. Discuss that task. Discuss also why it has not been undertaken and what could be done about it.

Lead the discussion to the level of the worldwide mission of the church, showing how our congregation, even though small, helps support the mission of the church in many other lands. Help the group understand that without having several congregations working together in many different places mission could never happen.

W E E K
NINE

First Day: Read Acts 18:24-28.

See: After Paul had left, the Alexandrian Jew Apollos arrived in Ephesus. Alexandria was famous for its schools and letters, and therefore it is not surprising that Apollos was a well-educated person. In verses 24-25 we are told many positive things about him. "He was an eloquent man, well-versed in the scriptures. He had been instructed in the Way of the Lord; and he spoke with burning enthusiasm and taught accurately the things concerning Jesus." But at the end of verse 25 we are told also that "he knew only the baptism of John." Exactly what this means is not altogether clear. Probably, although Apollos knew Scriptures and also the story of Jesus, he had not yet reached the conclusion that Jesus was the fulfillment of the promises made in Scripture. John's baptism was for repentance and, like any repentance, could be repeated as often as necessary. By contrast, Christian baptism was entry into a new era, a new reality. It was an act of becoming a citizen of the reign that had been inaugurated with Jesus and with the outpouring of the Holy Spirit. Constant repentance is still necessary, but one does not have to be baptized every time one returns to the community after having sinned, for Jesus fulfilled our redemption once and for all.

What is most interesting in this passage is that Priscilla and Aquila, whose erudition probably fell far short of that of Apollos, called him aside and taught him what he still needed to learn.

Judge: Eloquence is appreciated in most churches. Very few things attract us as much as a speaker whose words flow with beauty, precision, and harmony. In many churches there is appreciation for fervor, and therefore anyone who speaks both eloquently and fervently seems to have already all that is needful. There are many pastors, as well as many in the laity, who believe that fervor and eloquence are the two main characteristics of a good teacher of the faith. Apollos fulfilled these two requirements: He "spoke with burning enthusiasm" and "was an eloquent man."

However, that was not enough. He had to know "more accurately" the way of the Lord. This means that, in spite of the commonly held opinion, fervor and eloquence do not suffice. It is necessary to continue to know the way of the Lord more accurately.

This requires first of all a humble spirit that reminds us that, no matter how much we know, there is still much more to learn. We must be ready to learn not only from books and distinguished teachers, but also from people seemingly less schooled or less sophisticated. The pastor and the Sunday school teacher have much to teach, and deserve our attention. But so do other people who might seem to be less learned. If we listen to them with a humble spirit, we may be surprised at what we learn.

Act: Think of a brother or sister in church to whom you have not paid much attention, perhaps because he or she did not seem to be interesting or have much to say. Resolve to listen to that person, to ask his or her opinion whenever possible, to ask about his or her faith. Write down what you learn from such conversations.

Second Day: Read Acts 19:1-7.

See: This episode is closely related to the previous one. It took place after Apollos had left Ephesus, but apparently there were in the city some disciples who only knew of the baptism of John (verse 3). This is similar to the phrase that appears in 18:25 with reference to Apollos and therefore seems to imply a connection between these disciples and that teacher. Were they perhaps people who had heard Apollos teach before Priscilla and Aquila clarified the gospel to him? Or were they people from the same circle from which Apollos came? It is impossible to know.

At any rate, now we are told more about the deficiency, if not necessarily of Apollos, at least of these disciples. Paul added two things to what they already knew: First, that the preaching of John the Baptist pointed to the one who was coming after him, Jesus the Christ; and, second, that there is a Holy Spirit. Apparently, these disciples were followers of Jesus as a teacher but not as the Christ, the promised Messiah, the fulfillment of the promises. (Could this be also the deficiency in the teaching of Apollos, that he could teach with accuracy about the doctrines and miracles of Jesus but he did not know that he was the fulfillment of the promises?)

What Paul told them was that this was precisely the message of John himself. Then, on the basis of the joint witness of John and Paul, these twelve were baptized and, when Paul laid his hands on them, they received the Spirit.

Judge: Although this is not the place for developing the doctrine of the Spirit, there are two points that should be underscored in this narrative, and which are also important in our churches, where often there is so much talk of the Holy Spirit.

The first point is that there is a clear connection between having the Spirit and being able to confess fully who Jesus is. This is seen in the narrative itself. These twelve do not know about the Spirit, and Paul responds to that deficiency by telling them that Jesus is the Christ. Then they are baptized in the name of Jesus, and they receive the Spirit. In this particular case, when Paul learns that someone does not know of the Spirit, he responds to that need by speaking to them of Jesus. There is a close connection between knowing and confessing Jesus as the Christ and having the Holy Spirit. As Paul himself says in 1 Corinthians 12:3, "no one can say 'Jesus is Lord' except by the Holy Spirit."

The second point is that the manner in which all of this is related, and what events come first, is not always the same. We like to have everything down in black and white, to know exactly how, when, and where the Spirit acts. There are in some churches people who claim to know more about the Spirit's gifts and action than it is possible for humans to know. But that is an attempt to limit the power and freedom of the Spirit. Here, as in most parallel passages in Acts, the Spirit comes after baptism, with the imposition of hands by the apostles (see, for instance, 8:17). However, in the case of Cornelius that we studied a few days ago, the Gentiles received the Spirit first, without Peter laying his hands on them, and it is only later, as a consequence of having received the Spirit, that Cornelius and his friends are baptized.

The significance of this should be clear: Let us not claim to know more than we can really know, or to set orders and limits for the Spirit.

Act: If you have fixed ideas as to how, when, and where the Spirit acts, ask God to free you from such ideas. At any rate, pray for help to see the Spirit acting in various ways, in different places, and in different people. Write down your prayer in your notebook. Repeat it.

Third Day: Read Acts 19:8-10.

See: Today we are looking at a very brief passage. Almost in passing, we are told that Paul spent two years in Ephesus. When we read Acts, quite often we think that Paul was constantly moving from one place to another, and as soon as he was able to preach and gain a few converts in a town, he would leave for another. That is not true. Although the author mentions only the outstanding events in each particular place Paul visited, he also lets it be understood that, at least in some of those places, Paul remained for several months and even years.

Judge: Continued and persistent commitment is one of the most scarce virtues. If we ask for people to offer themselves for a task that will require significant sacrifice, hard work, and even serious risk, but must be completed in a week, it will be relatively easy to find volunteers. But if we ask people to commit to a task that will take years, even at less risk and level of work, it is much more difficult to find such volunteers.

This is seen almost daily in the life of the church. There usually is someone available for a difficult but short task. But if we ask volunteers who will commit to teaching in Sunday school, to prepare every Sunday to lead a productive session, and to do this for several years, we will be hard pressed to find enough people.

Furthermore, perhaps a heroic but brief effort is much more appreciated than one that requires a long-term commitment, even though it may be just as heroic. Thus, for instance, we often admire someone whose life was offered up in martyrdom, but we say little of a missionary who spent thirty years preaching and teaching before gaining even a first convert. We admire the evangelist who comes and preaches a good sermon, but not the pastor who spends years taking care of the flock, rising at midnight in order to respond to some need, helping parents in rearing their children, and comforting those who grieve over the loss of a loved one. The sad consequence of this is that, because they are not esteemed, these very people sometimes become discouraged because there is not a dramatic moment in their continued labor.

Act: How long has your pastor been serving in your church? How long since you last encouraged your pastor with a word of gratitude and support? Do it now.

Think of other people who have shown their commitment for years. Resolve to encourage them and to let them know that you appreciate their dedication and commitment.

Are you committed to a long-term task that springs out of your faith? If not, think and pray over the possibility of making such a commitment. Ask others in your church to provide you support and guidance in that task.

Fourth Day: Read Acts 19:11-16.

See: In verse 11 we are told of the miracles that were taking place in Ephesus, and of people coming to be healed. Some even took handkerchiefs or aprons that had touched Paul, and with them healed the sick.

However, what usually happens in such cases also happened here: There were those who tried to imitate Paul for their own ends. They sought to expel evil spirits by saying, "I adjure you by the Jesus whom Paul proclaims."

Among these people there were seven brothers, the sons of a priest called Sceva, who went to a man who was ill and tried to rid him of his disease by employing that formula. But the evil spirit mocked them saying: "Jesus I know, and Paul I know; but who are you?"

After this, the sick man jumped on them and gave them a sound thrashing.

Judge: What we see in the text is the tragedy of seven people who tried to face the power of evil by covering themselves with the name of Jesus. They wished to claim the power that Jesus seemed to have over evil, but not his power over their own lives. That is why their attitude is ridiculous and ineffective, to the point that the evil itself mocks them and humiliates them.

However, we should not be too quick to judge, for what those seven did is very similar to what we attempt to do quite often. When we have a problem, or when we wish to face a problem in our community, we claim the power of the Lord, asking him to intervene and to perform a miracle. But we are not quite ready to allow him to intervene in our lives, interrupting our purposes and doing with us as he will.

The main difference between Paul and these false exorcists was that Paul spoke of Jesus not by hearsay or from afar, but as one who had accepted the lordship of Jesus over his own life. By contrast, the seven sons of Sceva are not ready to claim such power over themselves, the very power that now they wish to apply to the demon. It is that which makes them ridiculous and powerless. The same happens to us when we seek to apply the power of Jesus to the rest of the world, or to a particular problem in our own lives, but are not willing to acknowledge that power in our entire lives.

But there is more. The demon acknowledged Jesus and Paul, but not the seven would-be exorcists. Why? Because both Jesus and Paul had repeatedly faced the power of evil. Jesus did not remain at the edges of evil, without knowing it or suffering it. On the contrary, he faced temptation in the desert; whenever he saw suffering or injustice he combated them; and finally on the cross directly faced the most terrible powers of evil. Paul followed his example. In the passages we have studied, we have seen him flogged, imprisoned, and stoned to the point that people thought him dead. Jesus and Paul had faced the powers of evil and had overcome, and that is why evil acknowledged them.

This is very important, because sometimes we think that if we are true Christians evil will not touch us. The truth is probably the opposite: If we are true disciples of the Lord of the cross, we shall actively face evil. Evil will know and acknowledge us. Evil will launch against us its most terrible weapons. Evil will make us suffer, but we shall overcome. This is what will make evil acknowledge us, rather than tell us, as it told those would-be exorcists, "Jesus I know, Paul I know; but who are you?"

This is precisely the reason that so often Christians and churches do not have the power we ought to have to defeat evil. We wish to defeat evil from afar, just as we wish to claim Jesus as Lord but also to keep him at a distance. And then we are surprised that evil laughs at us or simply ignores us!

We complain, for instance, of the rampant presence of violence and drugs in our neighborhoods. But what do we do about it? Our denominations make high-sounding declarations about violence and drugs. Our local churches declare themselves to be against violence and drugs. In our sermons we say that violence is bad, and that drugs destroy both the individual and the community. But where and when do we truly voluntarily face violence and drugs? We want the power of Jesus to solve the problem. But, how would Jesus face such a problem? How would Jesus want us to face it?

Act: Pray: "Our God and our Lord, who in Jesus has given us the power to overcome evil and even death, give us faith so as to follow Jesus, and so to allow him to rule our lives and our church, that we may also experience his power over all the evil that surrounds us. In his name I pray. Amen."

Fifth Day: Read Acts 19:17-20.

See: These four verses summarize the reaction of various groups to the events that have taken place, and especially to the outcome of the efforts at exorcism by the sons of Sceva. Verse 17 tells us that everybody in Ephesus, "both Jews and Greeks," was amazed. Verse 18 tells us that the news also affected Christians who "confessed and disclosed their practices." The next verse tells us about "those who practiced magic," although it is not clear whether these were Christians who still retained their magical practices or whether they were other people who heard what had happened. It probably refers to both, and therefore it is also quite likely that one of the sins that the believers confessed (verse 18) was retaining their old superstitions.

It is significant that these events took place in Ephesus, for that city was known by the books of magic it produced, which were often called "Ephesine Books." It is also important to understand the high price of the books that were destroyed. Fifty thousand pieces of silver would be about the salary of a person for as many days, or about one hundred and fifty years. Quite possibly the author gives us that figure in order to contrast this with the next episode, where economic interests would try to hinder the preaching of the gospel. However, the impact of that preaching is such that it overcomes every economic interest.

Finally, verse 20 is another of the "summaries" to be found in Acts.

Judge: The miracle that we studied yesterday affected not only Jews and Greeks but also those who had believed. Furthermore, it is quite possible that some of those who had believed were still practicing magic. Today, quite often we ask for signs that will convince those who do not believe, so that they may be converted. But let us not forget that God's revelation also reveals our own darkness. In this biblical account, Christians were moved to confess and to give an accounting for their actions. Also today, when God speaks to us, it is not only to reaffirm the position and attitude of those who believe over against unbelievers, but also to show us something of our own lack of faith, our own sin, our own need for forgiveness. When God speaks, we must be the first to answer; we must not think that God's presence will overwhelm only those who do not believe or who are outside the church.

If this very day you were to see a clear manifestation of God's power, what sins or dark corners of your life would you have to confess?

Act: Take some time to think about that question. Write down your answers in your notebook. Remember that right now, God is right there in front of you, whether you see miracles or not. Pray for forgiveness for those things that you have had to write down.

Sixth Day: Read Acts 19:21-22.

See: This brief passage is an outline of what is to come. Particularly in verse 21, we are told that Paul will go through Macedonia and Achaia, in order eventually to reach Jerusalem and finally Rome itself. In other words, this verse summarizes the rest of the narrative of Acts. However, what we have here is much more than a summary; it is an announcement of a radical change in the nature of the narrative. The phrase that the NRSV translates as "after these things had been accomplished" underlines that change. When something has been accomplished, it is time to move to something else. In a way, Paul had completed the first phase of the mission that the Spirit had entrusted to him. What was now lacking was going to Jerusalem and to Rome, which were not so much places of missionary work as they were places of suffering and persecution. In Paul's career, this passage is parallel to Luke's telling us that Jesus "set his face to go to Jerusalem" (Luke 9:51). In that verse in Luke the same word "to fulfill" is to be found. Just as in his Gospel, Luke still has much to tell us about Jesus before he actually reaches Jerusalem, so also here in Acts he still has much to tell us about Paul's mission.

Judge: We all face situations in which it is necessary to make difficult decisions that may result in extra work, difficulties, and even pain. A mother who has devoted long years to care for her children and for her home decides that now she will undertake a career, knowing that this will demand long years of study and sacrifice. A young man has to decide whether to accept a seemingly advantageous job offer that could perhaps require his involvement in dubious activities. A father has to punish a son, even though it pains him.

Some of those decisions are imposed on us by life itself. It is not possible to do or to have all that we wish. It is necessary to choose some things and to set aside others.

But there are also difficult decisions that result from our commitment to serve Christ. The day we put our hands to the plow, we chose a life that is not easy. Discipleship involves moments in which we too have to set our face to go to Jerusalem—that is, to undertake a difficult or costly task.

Have you ever faced such a situation?

Act: Just as Paul reached a turning point in his life, perhaps you are approaching a similar point. Review what you have been writing in your notebook. Ask in prayer: "Lord, what do you require of me?"

Continue praying about this, and asking the advice of others in the church, until you have an answer.

Seventh Day: Read Acts 19:23-41.

See: One of the wonders of the ancient world was the great Temple of Artemis in Ephesus. (Since the Greek Artemis has been equated with the Latin Diana, sometimes it was also called the Temple of Diana. In some older English versions of the Bible, the name used at this point is Diana.) This temple, besides being the pride of the city, was also an important source of income, for pilgrims from all over the Mediterranean Basin came to it. Also, as was customary in ancient times, it served as a bank that held the city treasury as well as deposits from private citizens.

The story is relatively simple. It all began with a silversmith named Demetrius and those who worked with him. Part of their business was to make small temples of silver, replicas of the great temple of Artemis, which pilgrims would take back with them as they returned home—very much as tourists today buy souvenirs.

Concerned over the economic loss that Paul's preaching might cause, Demetrius called together "the workers of the same trade" and incited them to action on the basis of a combination of economic self-interest and religious fervor. According to Demetrius, Paul's preaching had led many to abandon the worship of the gods, and therefore "there is danger not only that this trade of ours may come into disrepute but also that the temple of the great goddess Artemis will be scorned, and she will be deprived of her majesty that brought all Asia and the world to worship her." At this, his audience was enraged and began shouting "Great is Artemis of the Ephesians!"

Soon there was general confusion and the mob headed toward the theater, the most appropriate place in the city for popular assemblies and demonstrations. Along the way they grabbed two of Paul's companions, Gaius and Aristarchus, and took these two with them.

The theater of Ephesus was imposing. It was a vast semicircle built on the side of a hill and facing the sea, with marble seating for twenty-four thousand persons. At that time it was undergoing reconstruction in a series of works that continued till the beginning of the second century. When Paul learned what was happening, he tried to go to the theater himself, but "the disciples would not let him." In Romans 16:3-4, Paul said that Priscilla and Aquila risked their lives for him: "Greet Prisca and Aquila, who work with me in Christ Jesus, and who risked their necks for my life." Could he perhaps have been referring to something that took place during the riot in Ephesus? Could it have been this couple that kept Paul from going to the theater?

At any rate, in the theater the riot continued. In Acts 19:32, the author describes that confusion in brief words: "some were shouting one thing, some another; for the assembly was in confusion, and most of them did not know why they had come together."

Verses 33-34 reflect the same confusion, to such a point that it is difficult to know what was actually taking place. Who was this Alexander, who appears here with no other explanation? No one knows. What is clear, however, is that the pandemonium continued for over two hours, while people kept on shouting "Great is Artemis of the Ephesians!"

Finally, the "town clerk" intervened. That title does not reflect the full authority of this person, who in fact was the intermediary between Roman rule and the city assembly. It was on the basis of that authority that he managed to calm the mob. He began by telling them that it was not necessary for them to go about shouting about the greatness of their goddess, for "who is there that does not know that the city of the Ephesians is the temple keeper of the great Artemis and of the statue that fell from heaven?"

This notion of a statue coming down from heaven was the clerk's response to what Demetrius had said earlier regarding Paul's preaching against "gods made with hands." Since Artemis had fallen from heaven, she was not vulnerable to such criticism. Up to this point, the town clerk wisely told the populace that they were right. Then, however, the tone of his speech changed. Those who were rioting had broken the law, and the entire city was "in danger of being charged with rioting today, since there is no cause that we can give to justify this commotion." Rioting was considered a serious crime in the Roman Empire, and therefore the clerk's warning must have chilled even the most rowdy. At any rate, with those words the town clerk managed to disperse the mob.

Judge: This episode of the riot in Ephesus has so many apparently modern overtones that it could well have been written today, even though no one worships Artemis anymore and her famous temple is in ruins. What is most remarkable here is the way in which the narrative entwines economic and religious motivations. There are two dimensions to this story that are often repeated even today. First is that the silversmiths eventually were convinced that their shouting was due only to their religious fervor, not their economic motivation. The second is that soon there was an entire multitude of people shouting, without having the slightest notion of the reason for the riot or of the manner in which their shouts served the interests of Demetrius and his colleagues.

In the case of the riot in Ephesus, the intervention of Roman authority in the person of the town clerk helped Christians, for the riot was quenched. But that is not always the case. In John 11:48, the opposite happens. Jesus had just raised Lazarus. One would expect the religious leaders of the people to acknowledge and acclaim his power. But what they actually did was to gather in council and to reach the conclusion that they must seek to kill Jesus: "If we let him go on like this, everyone will believe in him, and the Romans will come and destroy both our holy place and our nation."

These leaders of Israel, just like the town clerk and just like many people today who are supposedly powerful, were not their own lords, and sometimes they acted one way and sometimes another, not according to truth but according to whatever seemed to best serve the interests of those who were above them.

Act: What are we to do in such a situation? There are at least three things we should do:

First, we must examine ourselves. Is it possible that, on some point or situation in which I am convinced that my attitude is due only to my sincere faith, in truth I am serving my own interests or those of others whom I wish to please?

Second, we are to be "wise as serpents." As Luke does in Acts, we must try to understand what is happening around us by analyzing and recognizing the powers and interests at play in the situation.

Third, and most important, we must be faithful among all those interests. Paul was a Roman citizen. But that did not lead him to befriend the Empire. No matter how much Caesar might have served as a protection to him, Paul's task was not to defend Caesar but to announce Jesus as a sovereign before whom every other lordship must give way. If that led to his being accused of subversion—as it did—such was the price of obedience.

In your notebook, make a list of the economic interests and the political obligations that seem to weigh on the church today. Then consider how those powers and obligations affect what the church says and does.

Discuss your conclusions with other people in your church. Together, try to discover the nature of obedience today and in the particular situations in which you find yourselves.

For Group Study

Choose an article in this week's newspaper discussing some problem in your community. Take it to the group and ask what are we to do as Christians in response to that problem. Write down the answers on newsprint or on a blackboard.

After allowing all to answer, ask the group to consider who would be upset if we were to take any of the actions suggested, and why that would be so. (For instance, if public transportation is insufficient and we begin a campaign to have it improved, those who now profit from offering private transportation would be upset.)

Toward the end of the session, remind the group of what they studied yesterday, about Jesus setting his face, and how Paul decided to go to Jerusalem and to Rome even though he knew that this would bring difficulties. Ask the class if it is not now the time when we should set our face and confront some of these situations in our own neighborhood.

W E E K
TEN

First Day: Read Acts 20:1-12.

See: The first part of the passage (verses 1-6) tells us something of the vicissitudes through which Paul had to go in his missionary task. On a map of Paul's journeys, follow his route at this point, and you will note that he had to return from Ephesus to Jerusalem by a very indirect route, in order to evade those who apparently sought to do him harm.

Then follows the episode of Troas, where Paul's preaching was so long that a young man called Eutychus fell asleep. Luke tells us that there were many lamps inside the room. At a time when the only light available was by means of fire, this would indicate that there was a lack of oxygen in the place, that the atmosphere became stuffy and even suffocating, and that this contributed to the young man's sleepiness.

What is really astounding in the passage is that, when Eutychus appeared to be dead and was raised up by Paul, the worship service continued as if nothing out of the ordinary had taken place. Communion was celebrated, and Paul went on teaching until morning.

Judge: Note the reactions of the church before the death and resuscitation of Eutychus. The first thing that happened was that the service was stopped, and Paul dealt with Eutychus and his urgent need. Sometimes in our churches we think that our services and our programs are so important that no matter what happens they are to go ahead, as if the condition of the society and those around us were unimportant. (This reminds us of the parable of the good Samaritan and the religious people who simply continued along their way.) What happened here was exactly the opposite. The agenda of the church was interrupted because someone was in need and it was necessary to respond to that need.

In our church, are we ready to interrupt our agendas for the needs of those around us?

Second, we are surprised at the reaction of the church to the resurrection of Eutychus. They rejoiced, but they returned to their worship service as if nothing much out of the ordinary had happened. Paul kept on preaching until dawn. Why? Certainly not because the miracle was not great, but because there was another miracle that was even greater—the life of the church itself, and the presence of God in its common life and in its breaking of bread. They reacted as they did, not because they did not realize the miracle by which Eutychus had been blessed, but because they were listening to the word of God, and the activity of that word is more miraculous, more powerful, more surprising, more amazing than the resurrection of a dead person.

The church is a miracle. That is the main theme of the entire book of Acts. It is a miracle that Jesus performs through the Spirit. If the church itself is not a miracle, if the life and action of the church are so routine that we need other miracles in order to confirm our faith, perhaps we need to rediscover the message of Acts about the activity of the Spirit in the church.

Act: Write in your notebook the following phrase, and complete it: "My church is a miracle because ___."

Complete that phrase in as many different ways as you can. Pray thanking God for all that you have been able to write and for the reality behind it. Resolve to share with others how the church itself is a miracle.

Second Day: Read Acts 20:13-38.

See: The events took place as Paul was traveling back toward Palestine, knowing that there he would have to face serious difficulties. Since he wished to reach Jerusalem by the Feast of Pentecost, he did not stop at Ephesus but rather took a ship to Miletus. (Follow this route on a map.) From there he sent for the leaders of the church in Ephesus in order to greet them and say farewell to them, for he did not expect to see them again. For that reason, this farewell was quite emotional.

Paul began his farewell by reminiscing. But then he brought his audience to the present. His own ministry was now approaching an end, and they were to continue his work. Therefore, verse 25 begins with the words "and now." These "elders" (verse 17) were now in charge of the church, to continue Paul's ministry, keeping the flock from "savage wolves" and other dangers.

Judge: One of the challenges that many of our churches have to face quite often is change in pastoral leadership. Often when a pastor leaves, there is a group that seems to believe that loyalty to the previous pastor is best expressed by not cooperating with the new one. On the other hand, there are also individuals and groups who make it a point of criticizing everything that was done before the arrival of the new pastor. Some don't like the new pastor's preaching. Others simply wish to erase all that was done before and start all over again. To make things worse, those who act in these various ways are precisely those who are supposed to be leaders in the church.

A good antidote against such attitudes would be to take this biblical passage very seriously. It is the Holy Spirit who is calling Paul to Jerusalem, but it is the same Spirit who will continue leading the church in Ephesus. The proof of the valor and faithfulness of the elders in Ephesus will be in their actions and attitudes when Paul is no longer among them. What this means for us is that one of the proofs of a true leader is that she or he takes care of the flock in every circumstance.

Are you that sort of leader?

Act: Consider your own faithfulness in the church. Does it depend on your agreement with what the pastor says or does? Does it depend on having other people praise you and make you feel good? Or is it based rather on your own faithfulness to Jesus Christ, so that you would continue being faithful even if you did not like the leadership of the church?

Write down your reflections. Pray for greater faithfulness.

Third Day: Read Acts 21:1-16.

See: In the section we are now studying, we enter the final section of Acts, where what Paul announced earlier will be fulfilled, that is, that he was going to Jerusalem where he would encounter chains.

In verse 10, we once again meet prophet Agabus, whom we have already found in Acts 11:28. Like the prophets of the Old Testament, he illustrated his prophecy by means of action. Tying himself with Paul's belt, he announced that the leadership in Jerusalem would tie Paul and "hand him over to the Gentiles." This is what will happen in the rest of the book.

Even though the prophet was clearly speaking under the Spirit's guidance, Paul's companions tried to persuade Paul not to go to Jerusalem. It was only after Paul had made it clear that he would go to Jerusalem that the rest said, "The Lord's will be done."

Judge: Do you find it surprising that, even though the Spirit spoke through Agabus, these Christians tried to dissuade Paul from going to Jerusalem? Perhaps the author is telling us that the Spirit acts in a very different way than we usually imagine. Our common understanding of the work of the Spirit is such that we expect to be left with no doubt, seeing clearly exactly what we are supposed to do. But perhaps the author of Acts, while insisting on the importance of taking the Spirit's directions seriously, is also telling us that we are not to take the Spirit as a crutch on which to lay our responsibilities for making difficult decisions.

In Acts, the Spirit does not tell Paul exactly what he is to do. On the contrary, the Spirit urges Paul to go to Jerusalem but also uses other people to warn him about the price of doing so. The final decision is still in Paul's hands. At first, this may seem to weaken or diminish the authority of the Spirit, but in fact it does exactly the opposite. We must remember that, even when the Spirit speaks and leads us, all our decisions expose us to the risk and ambiguity that are characteristic of every human action. We cannot hide behind the Spirit and simply claim that "the Spirit told me to do it." But, for the same reason, we cannot hide behind the lack of clear direction in order not to do anything.

Not seeing this is one of the reasons that in so many churches there is so little action. We imagine that when the Spirit speaks, we will know exactly what to do and to say. Therefore, when there are any doubts about what action to take or what word to say, we do and say nothing, waiting for the Spirit to speak. Had Paul followed that procedure, he would never have gone to Jerusalem.

Act: Write in your notebook: "Beginning today, I will no longer wait until all doubts are cleared before I act. I will ask for the direction of the Spirit; I will consult with others. Then, I will do whatever I believe that the Spirit is guiding me to do. I will take the risk of being wrong, but I will not take the risk of not doing anything."

Fourth Day: Read Acts 21:17-25.

See: Paul finally reached Jerusalem, where he was well received by the church. But, even though they welcomed him, they told him that there was a problem, since some among the Jews were saying that he was trying to persuade Jews to become Christians and to abandon the law of Moses. As we know, this was not true. But in spite of this, the leaders of the church in Jerusalem wanted Paul to offer public proof that what was being said of him was false. For this reason they suggested that he go to the Temple and there purify himself jointly with others who had made a vow. The expectation was that when they saw Paul doing these things, those Jews who were more zealous guardians of their traditions would be convinced that he was not intending to subvert or deny those traditions.

Judge: From this moment on, we will see Paul in the midst of various powers and interests that try to control and judge him. We will also notice that those powers and interests are very similar to those surrounding us today.

As we study today's passage, we see the pressure applied to Paul by the leaders of the church in Jerusalem, who were concerned that Paul's work might be misinterpreted. Someone was going around saying that Paul was inviting Jews to abandon the laws of Moses and those customs that were at the very heart of Jewish identity. James and the elders did not seem to give credit to such rumors, but they also did not seem to do much to quiet them. They did suggest some steps that Paul could take that they thought would belie those who misrepresented Paul and his mission. But they did not offer to go with him or to speak in his favor. Sadly, what we see here is the waning of that solidarity and sharing that was so prominent in the first chapters of Acts.

It is not necessary to look very far in order to find points at which this situation touches on the life of our churches today, where rumor and gossip are often powerful instruments of evil. We usually think that the problem lies only with the active gossipmongers. But the problem is much larger, for it involves also those who say that they do not believe the gossip but who still pass it on, or at least do nothing to contradict it.

There are even some who approach a brother or a sister and say: "You know? So and so is saying such and such about you." But they do not take the trouble to confront the person spreading the gossip. In that case, they too become gossipers. Rather than diminishing the power of the gossip already being told, they now add their piece to it, by speaking ill of the person telling it. In some ways, this is similar to what happened in the case of Paul and the leaders of the church in Jerusalem. Those leaders, instead of confronting the falsehood of what was being said about Paul, brought to him their own gossip about those who were speaking ill of him.

Act: On a sheet of paper, write down every piece of gossip that you have heard in the last few months about anyone in your church. Write down any gossip you yourself might have spread. Find a safe place and burn the piece of paper. Or shred it and throw it out. Resolve never again to repeat any gossip you may hear. Pray for strength to fulfill that resolution.

Fifth Day: Read Acts 21:26-30.

See: What happened when Paul presented himself at the Temple was the opposite of what the leaders of the church expected. Some Jews from Asia (that is, from Ephesus and the surrounding area), who already knew of the conflicts that had taken place in that other area, aroused the crowd in such a way that there was a general disorder, and the Roman tribune intervened and arrested Paul.

Judge: Another of the powers and interests that we now see around Paul is this crowd of Jewish believers. We can only imagine Paul's pain, not only at the physical tragedy of his imprisonment, but especially seeing that it is the Jewish people themselves who have turned him over to the Roman authorities, when it actually is "for the sake of the hope of Israel" (28:20) that he now finds himself in prison.

Similar tragedies have occurred frequently throughout the history of the church. There have been many who, precisely out of love for the church, have sought to reform it. They have usually been denied and rejected by the very church that they so loved. Rather than listening to what they had to say, the church expelled them as heretics. In some cases in the past, they have paid for their love for the church with their own lives.

Although today we no longer burn heretics at the stake, human nature and the nature of institutions is still the same. Quite often those who seek to improve the life of the church because they love it find themselves excluded, criticized, even forced out.

In some cases, the reaction is not so extreme. Someone who has been a leader for some time may propose something that is not popular, and the rest of the congregation pushes that person aside. Or a young person suggests a way of doing things, and the older generation reacts with deaf ears, attributing to the recklessness of youth what is in fact an expression of love for the church.

Act: Think of someone in your church or community who has been wrongly criticized for saying or doing something that was unpopular. Reflect on your own attitude toward that person. Pray for that person. If you feel inspired to do so, call that person and offer him or her some words of encouragement.

Sixth Day: Read Acts 21:31-40.

See: The disorder rose to the point that the entire city was in an uproar, and the tribune who was in charge of the Roman garrison heard of it. Later on we will be told that the tribune's name was Claudius Lysias. He was a "commander of a thousand" and was in charge of the Roman garrison in the city, whose headquarters were in a tower from which one could look into the courtyard of the Temple. Therefore, it would not have been difficult for the tribune to learn of the riot and to know that it was centered at the Temple. Perhaps he could even see from atop the tower who was at the heart of the uproar.

The tribune acted on false presuppositions, thinking that Paul was a certain "Egyptian" (that is, a Jew who was called by that name) who had become known for his subversive activities against Roman authority. (Those whom the NRSV calls "assassins" were nationalists who would surreptitiously stab Roman officials and those among the Jews who collaborated with them, and then disappear among the multitude.)

Paul shattered the man's prejudices by speaking to him in a refined form of Greek, showing that he was mistaken.

Judge: Among the powers and people surrounding Paul, there was a tribune. The tribune was seeking to defend his own interests and following his prejudices. His main concern was to make certain that Roman authority and the order imposed by Rome would not be undermined. His prejudice led him to think that everything that happened in Jerusalem had to do with that interest of his, and that anyone who caused a riot or disorder must be either the Egyptian or one of the assassins. But Paul surprised him by speaking to him in a very refined form of address, and forced him to rethink his prejudice.

Many of us have experienced prejudice in various ways. Sometimes it is racial or ethnic prejudice. Sometimes it is cultural prejudice. Sometimes it is religious prejudice that tries to label people and classify them into various groups.

There are many different ways of responding to prejudice. One of them is by violence. That is not what Paul did. Another is to accept the prejudices of the powerful, to try to act as they tell us to do, and to be as much like them as possible. But Paul did neither one nor the other. He responded to the tribune in a form of address that immediately showed that he was not the uncouth person that the tribune had imagined, and immediately he addressed the crowd "in the Hebrew language"—a language that probably the tribune did not understand and considered inferior to his own Latin or Greek.

There are still today many prejudices. There are prejudices within the church. There are people outside the church who hold prejudices about what Christianity is. Today once more we can respond to prejudice in various ways. Perhaps Paul can lead us in that decision.

Act: Have you ever experienced prejudice? From whom? How have you reacted? Was your reaction similar to Paul's in this passage? What can you learn from Paul on this point?

Write down your reflections.

Seventh Day: Read Acts 22:1-24.

See: Having received permission from Claudius Lysias, Paul addressed the crowd "in the Hebrew language"—that is, Aramaic. His speech was mostly autobiographical. It is here that we learn that Paul, although from Tarsus, had been raised in Jerusalem, and had studied "at the feet of Gamaliel," whom we have already met in 5:34-39.

It is also here that we have the second narrative in Acts of Paul's conversion. The other two such narratives are in 9:1-19 and 26:12-18. Verses 17-21 add something that we did not know to this point. In Jerusalem, precisely in the Temple, Paul had a vision in which Jesus told him to leave the city, "because they will not accept your testimony about me." It was at that point that Jesus told him: "Go, for I will send you far away to the Gentiles." Although the multitude listened to him up to this point, it is not surprising that they now became rowdy again. In these few words, Paul offended them doubly. In the first place, he declared that it was precisely here, in this holy place, that Jesus spoke to him. By claiming this, Paul was equating Jesus with the God to whom the Temple had been raised. Second, Paul once again mentioned his mission to the Gentiles, which was precisely the reason for the riot, and he affirmed that his mission was the result of a commandment received in the Temple.

Once again the crowd demanded that Paul be destroyed, and the uproar threatened to become a riot. In order to calm the situation, the tribune ordered the soldiers to take Paul into the fortress. (He was already on the stairs leading to it.) There he would seek the truth of the matter, having Paul flogged in order to get the truth from him.

Judge: This particular speech by Paul provides some significant guidance for our mission today. First of all, Paul acknowledged and even underscored the points of contact or even agreement between him and his audience, and even credited them for their religious perceptions and traditions. This approach is in sheer contrast to what some today understand by "evangelism," by which they mean the process of attacking and rejecting the traditions and culture of those who listen. It is quite different from a sort of preaching that used to be quite prevalent and is still heard in some churches, where people of different cultures and traditions are told that all they learned from their ancestors is to be rejected. In contrast, Paul affirmed the religiousness of those who heard him. And he did this not only in order to gain their goodwill, but also and above all because he truly respected that religiosity and those traditions. He certainly invited them to believe in Jesus, and eventually his insistence on the name of Jesus would be the main reason why the uproar against his preaching resumed. But Paul did not preach Jesus to them by telling them that they were worth nothing, that they were a bunch of heathens, that their culture and tradition came from Satan. His message was one of love and affirmation meant for those who persecute Christians.

In my own Hispanic culture, quite often Protestant missionaries came to us telling us that in order to be true Christians we had to turn our back on all the cultural and religious traditions of our ancestors, as if they had been recalcitrant atheists who knew nothing about the things of God, and as if in order to become a Christian one had to accept a foreign culture—that of the missionaries who first preached to us.

In more recent times, the church has learned that in various parts of the world God is already active even before the preaching of the gospel takes place. This means that the culture and traditions of various people should be affirmed except when they actually contradict the gospel.

Act: Think about the various cultures and traditions present in your church community. Does your church benefit from this great variety of perspectives and experience? Or does it simply ignore or suppress those who speak a different word or look different? How would your church be enriched if these other cultural traditions were also present?

Consider the possibility of planning a meeting with Christians of other cultures and traditions. Suggest that possibility to your church. Discuss how you can relate to those various traditions which are present within the community around you.

For Group Study

Ask all the members of the group to mention a custom or tradition of their ancestors that they consider valuable and that they would like to recover. Write these on newsprint.

Ask the same question about customs and traditions that they have seen among their neighbors or elsewhere. Write these down also.

Now ask the group how these various traditions can be incorporated into its life and into the life of the church. (For instance, if someone has mentioned some of the traditional ways of celebrating Christmas, how can we bring that into our common life today?)

Write down the answers. If the group shows interest, a small committee could be appointed to follow through with some of the suggestions.

WEEK
ELEVEN

First Day: Read Acts 22:25-29.

See: Lysias took charge of the situation, apparently in order to avoid a riot that could have been a stain on his career. As was customary, he planned to have Paul flogged in order to force him to tell what had been happening and why his presence had created such an uproar. (Torturing prisoners in order to force them to confess to a crime was a general practice at the time, and still is in some circles.) This is why they tied him with thongs, probably to a pole in the ground or to a ring on the wall.

But now Paul claimed his rights as a Roman citizen, and the centurion who was supposed to put Paul to the question ran to warn the tribune that he had been about to flog a Roman citizen. Surprised, the tribune asked Paul if he truly was a Roman citizen. And, to his even greater surprise, it turned out that Paul was a citizen by birth, whereas Claudius Lysias had bought his own citizenship. The result was that Lysias grew concerned over the possible consequences of his actions in arresting and trying Paul.

Judge: Even when in prison, Paul showed that he knew how to move amidst the political and religious powers of his time. Apparently, he was not particularly proud of being a Roman citizen. In the passage we studied two days ago, when Lysias asked Paul if he was not the "Egyptian," Paul responded that he was not, but was actually a citizen of Tarsus. However, in this other situation, when the Roman authorities were about to torture him with whips, Paul let them know that he was indeed a Roman citizen. The result was consternation among the very authorities that up to that moment thought that they had command of the situation. The tribune, who shortly before had thought that he had captured the famous "Egyptian" and probably expected a reward for his action, now found that his prisoner was a threat to his career.

Some Christians seem to think that Christian humility means we should not claim our rights. Such an attitude is particularly prevalent among recent immigrants to countries like the United States, or among other people who for other reasons are generally powerless in society, and who therefore think that not only as Christians but also as people lacking power and authority, they should remain silent and not protest even when their own rights are being trampled.

But the apostle Paul set a different example. As a Roman citizen, he had certain rights. Even though he did not use that citizenship to claim special privilege, he did claim it in order to demand justice and equity.

Likewise, Christians who have been taught always to be humble and quiet have to learn how to claim their rights when they are set aside. And most especially, we also have to learn how to claim the rights of others.

Act: If in your community there are immigrants or other people who suffer discrimination, take whatever steps are necessary so that your church may welcome and empower them. Consider the possibility of an educational program to let them know of their rights, as well as an advocacy program to make sure that those rights are respected.

Second Day: Read Acts 22:30–23:10.

See: On the following day, Lysias called together "the chief priests and the entire council" in order to find out what were the accusations against Paul. This was probably not an official session of the council, but rather a gathering of the members, called together by the tribune and meeting in his residence. Since it was not an official meeting of the council, one may suppose that Ananias was not wearing the vestments corresponding to his high office, nor was he presiding at the session. One should also suppose that the discussion took place in Greek, or that there were translators present so that the tribune might know what was being said and discussed. After all, the purpose of the meeting was for him to be informed.

In verse 6 Paul astutely divided his accusers. Claiming his status as a Pharisee, he also claimed that what was being debated was "the hope of the resurrection of the dead." He did not explain further that what was really being discussed was not whether the dead would be resurrected, but rather if that resurrection had already begun with Jesus of Nazareth. At any rate, the result was that the members of the council were divided among themselves, and there was a heated debate between the Pharisees and the Sadducees precisely because this was one of the points in which the doctrine of the Pharisees was closer to Christianity than was the teaching of the Sadducees (verse 8). Apparently, the debate became so heated that the tribune began to fear for Paul's safety. Perhaps remembering that Paul was a Roman citizen, the tribune ordered his soldiers to intervene, to take Paul from amidst the debaters, and to return him to the fortress.

Judge: Once again Paul showed that he was politically astute. Rather than entering into a fruitless discussion with the members of the council, he made use of the disagreements he knew they had among themselves so that in the end they were debating each other rather than accusing him.

Throughout this study we have seen how various interests and powers oppose Christianity, and how they also oppose much good that the church can do. It is important to know and understand this, for otherwise we will be surprised and disheartened when we see that there are powers and interests opposing something that seems to us to be very good and even necessary.

In order to deal with such concerns, we have to try to understand those who oppose us, because frequently they do this for different and even contradictory reasons. When that is the case, it is possible to divide them and thus to weaken their opposition. This is what Paul did with the Pharisees and Sadducees in the council.

Think about a program in which the church has met opposition. What was the reason for that opposition? Did all the people who opposed this particular program have the same reasons? Or were there differences among them that we could have used in order to weaken their opposition, as Paul did before the council?

Act: Write down your reflections. Resolve to share them with others. If you cannot come up with an example of the sort of situation described above, ask others in your church if they know of such situations. This should result in a valuable conversation about the powers and interests that are at play in your community.

Third Day: Read Acts 23:11.

See: For today's study, we have centered our attention on a single verse. Note that, although the Lord invited Paul to keep his courage, he was not told that everything would turn out all right or that he would have no more problems. On the contrary, what the Lord told him was that what would happen in Rome would be similar to what had just happened in Jerusalem. In other words, he was told that his problems and difficulties were not ended but rather were about to become worse. And in spite of that, he was to keep his courage.

Judge: Commonly, when we try to encourage someone, we say something such as "Don't worry. Things are going to get better soon." But the Lord told Paul exactly the opposite. The Lord told Paul that he was to keep his courage, not because things were about to improve, but rather because difficulties would continue for quite some time.

When we stop to think about this, we realize that it makes sense. The apostle needed courage precisely because there were even greater difficulties ahead. The Lord encouraged him, not so that he might leave aside the task commended to him, but rather that he might have the strength necessary to fulfill it.

When we pray in the midst of difficulties, what do we ask for? Do we ask only that our problems be solved? Or do we ask rather that we may have the courage to face any difficulties that might arise out of our Christian obedience?

Throughout this study, we have frequently found Christians having problems and difficulties precisely because they were faithful. Remember the case of Peter and John before the council.

In such cases, what we are to ask is not that all our problems be solved or set aside, but rather that we may have the strength to remain faithful even in the midst of difficulties.

Act: Pray: "I don't ask, Lord, that you solve all my problems. I ask that you make me faithful. And if that creates difficulties for me, I ask that you give me courage to face those difficulties and remain faithful."

Copy that prayer in your notebook, and resolve to repeat it whenever you encounter difficulties in your life. Ask for this sort of courage, not only for yourself, but also for the church.

Fourth Day: Read Acts 23:12-15.

See: We are now told about a plot to kill Paul. It is an intrigue worthy of a modern spy novel. A fanatical group committed itself to fasting until they killed Paul, and then they recruited "the chief priests and elders."

The plan was rather simple. The priests and elders would ask the tribune to send Paul to appear before the council, and those who had sworn to kill him would fulfill their oath while he was being taken to the council through the narrow streets of Jerusalem. More than forty men joined the conspiracy.

Judge: For a number of reasons, we have become quite used to thinking and acting as if the church and Christians live beyond the political currents and intrigues of their time. Thus, for instance, when we talk about the story of a particular congregation, we remember who were the founders, where the first service was held, who were the first to join, and so on. All of that is important. But it is also important to remember that, from the very moment of its founding, each congregation existed in a concrete reality in the midst of a community in which, as in any community, there were different and conflicting interests and movements.

Whether we know it or not, those interests and movements affect the life of the church. Sometimes, as in the case of this conspiracy to kill Paul, they seek to hinder or to destroy the church. On other occasions, as we shall see later on, they are supportive. But in either case, they are always present.

Ask yourself:

What interests, conflicts, groups, and movements are there in my community, and how do they affect the life of the church?

Are we aware of these things, as Luke was when he wrote Acts?

Act: Go over the news that the media has reported the last few days about your neighborhood or city. Make a list of the main characters mentioned in that news (good, not so good, powerful, weak, and so forth). Walk or drive around your neighborhood, noticing the various businesses present, the sources of employment, banks, and so on. Then write in your notebook a page describing the various forces acting upon life in your neighborhood.

Resolve to discuss these matters with other people in church so that you may all come to a better understanding of how the witness of the church is received or rejected and why, as well as whose support and whose opposition the church can expect in its various actions.

Fifth Day: Read Acts 23:16-22.

See: The "novel" continues. Paul's nephew learns what is afoot. This is one of only two occasions in which Paul's family is mentioned in the New Testament (the other is Romans 16:7). It is only by this reference that we know that Paul had a sister.

At any rate, in his imprisonment Paul received the visit of this nephew, who told him what was being planned. Paul took good care not to say a word to those who guarded him. Rather, he asked one of the centurions to take the nephew before the tribune. Once the latter learned what was being plotted, he told the young man to keep silent and made plans in order to foil the conspiracy.

Judge: Yesterday we learned about a conspiracy against Paul. Now the plot thickens, for we learn of another plot (or counterplot) to save him. Out of nowhere, for we have never heard about him before, Paul's nephew comes into the picture. Tribune Claudius Lysias takes charge of the counterplot, even though he really is not terribly concerned about Paul's life. But he knows that if his prisoner is killed as the plotters are planning, this will be a blot on his career. Therefore, the interests of Paul's nephew in saving his uncle's life join the interests of the tribune in saving his own career.

The same thing happens quite often in the life of the church. While there are those who plot against it and its work for all sorts of reasons, there are also those who work and support it for their own reasons, which are often quite extraneous to the mission of the church. This episode in the book of Acts sets an interesting and valuable example, for Paul is quite willing to accept the tribune's help, even though he knows that such help will be given for personal and self-seeking reasons.

Act: In the list you made yesterday, there must be some elements that could be supporters of the church, at least in some aspects of its work. Make a list of these, and be ready to seek their help, or to convince other members of the church to seek their help, although at the same time being careful not to compromise the integrity of the gospel. Share these thoughts with other people in your church.

Sixth Day: Read Acts 23:23-32.

See: The plot and counterplot finally evolved. Although the plot was derailed, this did not mean that there would no longer be opposition from the religious leadership in Jerusalem. That opposition would reappear soon. But at least the plot of the forty who sought to kill Paul on his way to a meeting of the council was quite undone.

Astutely, Claudius Lysias decided to frustrate the plot of Paul's enemies and at the same time to rid himself of the problem by sending the prisoner to Caesarea under heavy guard. The situation had become too complex and dangerous, and the tribune, as quite often is the case with officials in any government, decided that the time had come to place the responsibility on somebody else's shoulders.

The letter that Lysias wrote was required by Roman legal practice when an inferior magistrate transferred a case to another above himself. The prisoner had to be accompanied by a document summarizing the process that had been followed and explaining the nature of the case to be tried. Claudius Lysias, as required by protocol, called governor Felix "his Excellency." That is the same title that the author of Acts gives Theophilus in 1:3.

It is interesting also to note that Lysias put a different twist on events, trying to avoid any possible criticism of his behavior. In verse 27, he claimed that he went to Paul's aid after he "had learned that he was a Roman citizen." According to the narrative in Acts, that is not quite true. Lysias went for other reasons, without even knowing who Paul was, and it was only much later that he learned that he was a Roman citizen. Note also that Lysias implied that Paul was innocent, but even so he sent the prisoner to be judged by Felix. It is not difficult to read between the lines and see the anxiety of a government official who feared the possible consequences of a situation and decided to pass the problem on to another.

Judge: Note that the fact that Lysias saved Paul from a very difficult situation did not lead the author of Acts to present that support naively. Note also that throughout this entire episode what Acts shows is Paul's political astuteness. The apostle is not presented, as we often imagine him, as a fiery preacher who continually charged against God's enemies, no matter who they might be or what their interests might be. On the contrary, he is depicted as a wily missionary who knew how to direct and use the various interests of each of the individuals involved. At the same time, he is also depicted as a man of integrity who was not ready to prevaricate or to remain silent simply to save his life.

This point is very important in our churches today, for quite often we err in thinking that because someone is helping us, that person is a Christian whom we should support no matter what. That is often the case with politicians who become champions of one or two causes of interest to Christians in order to court their votes. Sadly, quite often those very politicians are quite corrupt, and there is much in their political programs that is opposed to the love and justice that the gospel proclaims.

Act: Review some of the debates that took place during the last elections—or, if there is now a political campaign going on, the debates that are currently taking place. Look particularly at candidates who present themselves as defenders of "Christian values" or who have the support of any sort of "Christian coalition." Are they truly worthy of the unconditional support of Christians?

Write down your conclusions and share them with other people in your church. Make certain that your vote is not guided by easy promises or by empty slogans.

Seventh Day: Read Acts 23:33-35.

See: During this week we have been studying the lot of Paul under a Roman officer, the tribune Claudius Lysias, who was stationed in Jerusalem. Now Paul is handed over to a higher official, governor Felix, who resides in Caesarea. Paul will continue under the custody of Felix until Acts 24:27, when he will become the responsibility of Porcius Festus. That will be his condition until Acts 27:1, when he will leave for Rome, now under the care of centurion Julius. Finally, in Acts 28:16, Julius will hand Paul over to the military prefect of Rome. Therefore, all of these last chapters of Acts refer to a series of government officials who have no idea what to do with Paul or with this new phenomenon that is Christian teaching.

Back to the verses that we are studying today, we note that they tell us about how Paul was received in Caesarea and his first interview with Felix. Much is known about Felix through data preserved by Roman historians as well as by the Jewish historian Flavius Josephus. He was a freedman (that is, a slave who had been made free) whose brother had been a favorite of Agrippina, Nero's mother. Referring to the origins of Felix, historian Tacitus says that "he practiced all sorts of cruelty and lasciviousness, using the power of a king with the spirit of a lackey." One of the tactics that he used in advancing his career was to marry influential women, and for these reasons Suetonious calls him "the husband of three queens." Later on (Acts 24:24) we will hear of one of them, Drusilla. He was named procurator of Judea toward the end of the reign of Claudius, who died in the year 54. Thus, when Paul appeared before him, Felix had already held his post for some four years.

Felix inquired from Paul what province he was from, because before deciding whether to hear the case or not he had to determine the matter of jurisdiction. The Roman governors of Judea knew quite well that religious matters were thorny and could lead to riots that would not be considered favorably in Rome, where they would appear as signs of a governor's ineptitude. Therefore, if Felix could find a way to rid himself of this difficult case in which the religious leaders of Jerusalem were opposed to a Roman citizen, he would gladly do so.

An easy way to reach that objective would be to transfer the case to another province. A criminal case could be heard before the tribunals of the province in which the crime had been committed, or before those in the province of the accused. If Felix could transfer the case to Paul's province, he would have rid himself of a difficult matter. It turned out, however, that Paul, a native of Cilicia, was a citizen of Tarsus, a free city in that province, and therefore he was not subject to provincial authority. At least, that is how most scholars understand verses 34-35.

"Herod's headquarters," where Paul was kept under guard, was the ancient palace of Herod the Great, which served also as the headquarters of the Roman procurator, and which was sometimes called the "praetorium."

Judge: During this week, and throughout our study of Acts, we have noted that the author is quite realistic when it comes to the political, economic, and social powers that affect the ministry of the church. Such a realistic attitude requires that these powers be understood as both positive and negative. In Acts we see that the political, economic, and social interests of various people are opposed to the teaching of the gospel (the Jewish leaders in the first chapters, Demetrius and the silversmiths in chapter 19). At other times, those interests support the church or at least allow some leeway for its preachers (Gamaliel in the council, the city clerk in Ephesus, Lysias in what we have studied this week). In either case, Acts is realistic and sober in its judgment. It tries to understand the motivations of those who oppose the church, as well as the motivations of those who support or defend its leaders. It shows no bitterness toward the enemies, or adulation toward the powerful who for some reason protect the church or its teachers.

What could be more relevant than this assessment for our churches today?

On the one hand, there is a need for a realistic and sober political analysis. We need to know who the players are, what are their interests, what moves them. On the other hand, while we use such knowledge, we must do it with integrity. Between those two poles, the church often forgets the example of the apostle Paul. There are those who think that it suffices to "preach the gospel," forgetting that the gospel is always preached to human beings who live within a social and political context, and this context has much to do with how we are heard and how people react to what we say and do. Political and economic interests are quite ready to use Christians and the church, and they will do so for their own purposes if we do not know whose those interests are and what their goals are.

Sometimes we are too ready to play the game with whoever happens to be in power—in some countries the current dictator, in some other cases the rich person who offers money. Sometimes we are too willing to remain silent before injustice or oppression in exchange for the freedom to preach as we wish. Or we "sweeten the pill" to the rich so that they will not be offended and will continue giving their important offerings. However, between these two apparently opposed attitudes, the example of Paul rises as a challenge to wisdom and integrity. May God give us such leaders in the difficult times in which we live!

Act: Review what you have written in your notebook during this week. Note that, although on other occasions we have centered our attention on our own personal life, during this week we have been looking at the realities around our own life both as individuals and as a church. This perspective requires that, as believers, we begin analyzing those realities, not only individually, but as a group.

Gather a group of people (perhaps a Sunday school class, the group that is following this study, a youth group, or some other) and discuss with that group what we have been studying. The purpose is that, from now on, whenever the church has to make a decision, we consider these powers and interests about which Acts is so realistic.

For Group Study

Ask each person in the group to describe a particular section of your neighborhood or city. In those descriptions, point out and write down some of the powers and interests in whose context the church must carry forth its mission (for instance, banks, merchants, drug dealers, workshops, schools, police stations, and so forth).

Make a list of all these. Ask the group, in the light of what we have been studying this week, where they would expect some of these groups or individuals to support us, and where we can expect that they will be opposed to the mission of the church. If time allows, suggest to the group that they imagine a story similar to that of the apostle Paul, but having in this case the protagonist be a preacher who comes to our neighborhood speaking about Jesus and also about the need for justice for all. How would those interests that we have listed respond?

W E E K
TWELVE

First Day: Read Acts 24:1-21.

See: The passage is composed mainly of two speeches: that of the attorney hired by Ananias (who is not to be confused with the disciple by the same name who went to see Paul in Damascus, or the one who jointly with his wife lied to the church) and Paul's speech.

Paul's speeches begin, as was then customary, with some words of respect for the judge. In the manuals of speechmaking of the time, this beginning was called the "winning of benevolence"; in other words, its purpose was to win the goodwill of the judge.

Note, however, the contrast between the two speeches. Tertullus's was full of adulation: "Your Excellency, because of you we have long enjoyed peace, and reforms have been made for this people because of your foresight." In contrast, Paul simply says that "for many years you have been a judge over this nation." The truth is that Felix was a cruel and immoral man, as is attested by several authors of the time. Therefore, Paul's moderation is more truthful than the adulation of Tertullus.

It is also interesting to note the relationship between Tertullus's accusations and Paul's defense. Tertullus said that Paul was:

1. "a pestilent fellow"
2. "an agitator among all the Jews throughout the world"
3. "a ringleader of the sect of the Nazarenes"
4. someone who attempted "to profane the Temple"

Of all these charges, the only two that could have been interesting to Felix as a Roman judge are the second and the fourth.

Being accused of sedition or rioting was a very serious matter in the Roman Empire, and Felix would have been very much interested in avoiding profanations of the Temple that might lead to a riot. The first charge was merely an insult, and Paul completely ignored it. He did respond to the more serious accusations by denying them, saying that he was neither seditious nor a promoter of riots. Then he made use of the third charge, which in fact had no legal weight, to give a witness and to explain something of the nature of his faith.

Judge: Often Christians, like Paul before Felix, have to face corrupt or unworthy authorities. Sometimes it is someone who is unfair, unjust, or immoral. Most often it is simply a bureaucrat who enjoys abusing power. On other occasions it is someone who has authority within the church (a supervisor, a bishop or someone else with executive powers). Quite often we have no power to change such authorities, and therefore we have to deal with them. In such cases, Paul's example is worthy of imitation at least on the following three points.

First, Paul avoided adulation. He did not say a word that was not true, even though by praising his judge he could have gained greater goodwill.

Second, insofar as he could do this while respecting justice and truth, Paul respected authority. He did not tell Felix that, since he was corrupt and cruel, his authority was worthless.

Third, Paul found a way of getting to the crux of the matter, which was the gospel of Jesus Christ.

When we face such authorities, do we praise them excessively? Do we insult them? Do we witness to our faith?

Act: Review in your mind your last interview or encounter with a person who had authority or power over you. If you had followed Paul's example, would the experience have been different? Write in your notebook how you believe you should have responded.

Second Day: Read Acts 24:22-27.

See: What Felix did was simply to delay a decision, apparently with two purposes: to see if he could get some money from Paul and to improve his standing with Paul's enemies. Luke tells us that Felix "was rather well informed about the Way." Possibly this means not that he knew the doctrines of Christianity but simply that he knew how the new movement had been growing and the conflicts that had arisen in Jerusalem as well as elsewhere. At any rate, in order to delay matters, Felix used the excuse that he had to await a personal report from Lysias, and thus simply postponed a decision. However, at the same time he ordered that Paul be given a measure of freedom.

The interview of Paul with Felix and Drusilla is interesting. Drusilla was a younger daughter of Herod Agrippa the First (see Acts 1), and therefore a sister to Agrippa the Second and to Bernice (Acts 25:13). Their relationship with Felix had been turbulent and was one of the reasons that Felix was reputed to be a libertine.

At any rate, when Paul began to speak to them about "justice, self-control, and the coming judgment," Felix became frightened. Apparently he felt that Paul was hitting too close to home, for all indications are that Felix was not particularly known for his justice or self-control, but exactly the contrary.

Judge: The situation that is described here must have tried Paul's patience. He spent two years in prison, probably in chains, awaiting the result of a trial that had already taken place. Such a long period is even longer for one who knows that he is in prison simply because his judge is too weak to pronounce a verdict or is awaiting a bribe. During those years, Paul had the opportunity to practice what he himself had taught: "We also boast in our sufferings, knowing that suffering produces endurance, and endurance produces character, and character produces hope, and hope does not disappoint us" (Romans 5:3-5).

The lesson for us is clear. We are living in times in which Christian living requires, jointly with a holy impatience with injustice, an equally holy patience to persevere even when it seems that the present difficulties and sufferings have no end or solution. It is not a matter of simply adapting to the present situation. But it is also not a matter of becoming disheartened because our efforts do not produce immediate results. Paul was in the prisons of the most powerful empire that the Mediterranean world had ever known, and subject to the whims of a governor who was politically powerful and morally weak. There was ample reason to despair. But the years went by, and so did the centuries, and of that governor, of that empire, and of all their legions, there remains only a distant echo in the pages of history, while of the poor prisoner who seemed to wilt in the prisons of the Empire, people speak in every corner of the world, and his message resounds today with the same vibrant tone that frightened the weak and corrupt governor.

Act: When you feel impatient because of the manner in which evil and injustice seem to reign, remember the situation of those early Christians as they faced the Roman Empire. Write down in your notebook a situation that currently seems a good cause for despair. Now try to imagine what that situation will seem to you five years from now. Write down your thoughts. Ask God to help you face even the most disheartening situations with patience and with hope.

Third Day: Read Acts 25:1-12.

See: As a government official, Porcius Festus was the opposite of Felix. While his predecessor delayed Paul's legal process as much as he could, Festus moved toward a decision as quickly as possible. Three days after having arrived in his official residence in Caesarea, he was already in route to Jerusalem. There the religious leadership ("the chief priests and the leaders of the Jews") presented their charges against Paul. In little more than a week, Festus was already back in Caesarea, where he decided to hear the charges against the prisoner. Acts gives no details, and one can imagine that the charges now presented were similar to those that Tertullus presented two years earlier before Felix.

(Note that there were still some Jews who wanted to have Paul brought to Jerusalem, not so much that he might be tried there, but rather so that they might once again plot to kill him along the way.)

Even though he was an energetic governor, Porcius Festus knew that it was important to have the goodwill of the governed. Therefore, "wishing to do the Jews a favor," Festus suggested to Paul the possibility of going to Jerusalem and being tried there.

It was then that, in a solemn and dramatic gesture, Paul appealed to Caesar. From that moment on, other authorities and Roman judges had no jurisdiction over the case. They would be in charge of guarding Paul as a prisoner and taking him to Rome.

Judge: Festus, like Felix before him, was aware of the danger to his political career involved in granting freedom to this prisoner who is so hated by the Jewish leadership. It was this that led Paul to appeal to Caesar. This did not mean that Paul felt any particular preference or liking for the emperor, who at the time was the well-known Nero. What it meant was simply that Paul was aware of the inner contradiction between the legal principles that Festus was supposed to be defending, and the political interests that in fact determined his actions.

Such situations are still common. In many of our cities minority pastors have to deal daily with cases in which somebody in the police or in another branch of government violates the rights or the dignity of people, and the only way to have justice done is by appealing to higher authority.

What we often forget, and what is quite important, is that such cases are themselves a witness. In appealing to the emperor, Paul was pointing out, even though indirectly, the sad corruption of the Empire and the need for the message he proclaimed. He was not necessarily saying that the authorities were morally good. He was rather underscoring the inner contradiction of the system and demanding that at least it follow its own rules.

When a Hispanic pastor or an African American pastor files a complaint against a police system that seems to discriminate systematically against minorities, something similar is taking place. Taking action against discrimination shows the inner contradictions of the system, partly so that justice may be done and partly so that people may see the sort of life that the gospel requires and produces.

Act: Think of some individual or group in your neighborhood who suffers injustice. (This could be you yourself, the group to which you belong, a woman who is abused by her husband, a student who is being humiliated by teachers.) Write down the name of that person or group, as well as those who practice and support injustice. Now think about who or what is above that person or group. Write it down. (This higher authority could be the principal of the school, the laws of the land, or even the Constitution.) Consider how you and the church can uncover the injustice that is taking place, and use those higher powers to oppose it. Write down your reflections and share them with others who may join you in this task.

Fourth Day: Read Acts 25:13-27.

See: Technically, Paul was no longer under the jurisdiction of Felix as a judge. However, Felix was still responsible for making sure that he reached Rome.

The two who are simply called "King Agrippa and Bernice" were well known, among other things, for their licentiousness. This Agrippa is Herod Agrippa the Second, the son of Herod Agrippa the First (the same Herod who ordered that James be killed, and who was later eaten by worms, according to Acts 12). He was Drusilla's brother, therefore a brother-in-law to Felix. Bernice, who accompanied him, was his sister, as well as Drusilla's.

Bernice was famous for her immorality. She had first been married to a Jewish official in Alexandria, and then to her own uncle. When he died, she went to live with her brother Agrippa, and rumors about incest soon circulated. In part to quiet those rumors, she married the king of Cilicia. But she soon abandoned him and returned to live with her brother. After the events told here (but before Luke wrote the book of Acts) she became the lover of Titus, son of the emperor, who dropped her when he in turn became emperor. Thus, when Luke mentions Agrippa and Bernice, his readers would be well aware that this was not a very respectable couple.

The two went to Caesarea to visit Festus, a visit of protocol. It was in the midst of that visit that Agrippa showed curiosity about Paul and his case, and Festus brought the apostle before a rather fatuous audience.

Sometimes those who have power over others oppress them, not directly, but by turning them into mere objects of curiosity. Festus used Paul to amuse his guests Agrippa and Bernice. Is there any greater dehumanization than being turned into an object of curiosity, as is done with freaks in a circus? The problem is that, as Agrippa and Festus soon discovered, the supposed object of curiosity is still human, and that in the case of Paul he also had the power and conviction given him by the Holy Spirit.

Quite often, minorities become sources of folkloric amusement. There are people who do not really wish to learn anything about the culture and experiences of others, but do wish to listen to their music or eat their ethnic foods.

Sadly, this view is often found in the church. The majority church is interested in minorities because they sing fervently, because their music is different, or because their worship services are lively. It is good that they are interested in all these things. But if such interest does not go beyond curiosity about superficial matters and is only a source of amusement, that too is oppressive and dehumanizing.

Act: If you belong to an ethnic or cultural minority, think about these matters, and the next time you are invited to present your own culture before the dominant group do so, not as a matter of curiosity for them, but rather as something that the majority group actually needs. If, on the other hand, you belong to the dominant culture or ethnic group, make certain that next time you approach a different culture you do so really trying to learn something and not simply turning it into an object of curiosity.

Fifth Day: Read Acts 26:1-23.

See: Paul's speech began, as was customary at the time, with a few words in which he sought the goodwill of Agrippa. He told Agrippa that he rejoiced being before someone who actually knew the Jewish laws. Most likely the Apostle knew all that was being said about the immoral life of Agrippa and his sister, who were not particularly concerned over the laws of Israel. However, Paul spoke to them about those laws and, by taking for granted that Agrippa knew them, he indirectly told him that he ought to obey them.

There followed a testimony in which Paul told the basic facts of his life, underscoring his own Jewish background, how he had always been a faithful traditional Jew, even to the point of persecuting Christians. This gave him the opportunity to tell the story of his conversion (see Acts 9:1-19; 4:4-16).

The central theme of Paul's witness was that what he had done and what he taught did not contradict Moses and the prophets but, on the contrary, was the fulfillment of what they promised. This included the two central issues that led others to attack Christians: the announcement that the Messiah had come, and that he had risen from the dead.

Judge: Paul began his speech with words that showed his respect for King Agrippa. This may be surprising in light of what we know about Agrippa's immoral life. One would have expected the Apostle, who knew that after all the king could no longer harm him (for he had appealed to Caesar), to begin his speech by speaking of the immorality of his audience. But he began by showing respect even to such as Agrippa and Bernice.

Here is an important lesson for us. Some Christians are so zealous in their effort to share the gospel, and so enthused with the new life they have received, that they do not even notice that they approach others in disrespectful ways. In such cases, we approach such people seeing them not as people for whom Christ died, but rather as unrepentant sinners or ignorant idolaters who have to be convinced by means of insults. Such a witness, even when it may speak the truth, is not an announcement of the love of God.

Act: Think of someone you know who is not a believer. If possible, think about someone whose life leaves much to be desired. Now try to think about something of value in that person, something that you can say praising that person, and without hypocrisy. Write down what you have thought, and resolve, the next time that you see this person, to begin the conversation with these words of praise and respect, before offering an invitation to accept the life that there is in Christ.

Sixth Day: Read Acts 26:24-32.

See: Festus's response to Paul's witness was mockery: Paul is crazy, he is delirious. Even so, Festus did acknowledge Paul's wisdom: It was this "much learning" that was driving him insane.

Agrippa's answer was very similar, although sometimes it has been interpreted otherwise. The most common interpretation seems to understand that Agrippa was about to be converted. But in the original Greek there is a tone of mockery and irony, so that what Agrippa said could actually be translated: *With your arguments, you practically make me appear as a Christian.* In other words, Agrippa was saying that Paul had managed to make it look as if even Agrippa would have to become a Christian. An adequate paraphrase would be: *Paul, you almost managed to turn me into a witness in favor of Christianity.*

Paul's answer showed his Christian conviction. In spite of all the showiness of Agrippa and those who surrounded him, Paul had no reason to envy them, but was convinced that it was he who had the advantage except for his condition of being a prisoner: "I pray to God that not only you but also all who are listening to me today might become such as I am—except for these chains."

Judge: When we look around ourselves, we see many who are richer, more powerful, better educated, or more respected than ourselves, and therefore it is very easy to begin feeling sorry for ourselves. However, we must remember that we are daughters and sons of the Ruler of the universe, and therefore royal princes and princesses. This is why Paul could show respect toward Agrippa and also stand firmly before him. Agrippa might well be the king of a small piece of land in Palestine; but Paul was a child and a messenger of the supreme King. If we are truly convinced of this, we can face all people, no matter how rich or how poor, how powerful or how powerless, showing them the respect they deserve. But at the same time we will speak with the assurance and firmness that come only from knowing ourselves to be heirs of the celestial King.

Think about some particular occasion on which you have given witness to the gospel, and consider the following questions:

Did you show respect toward the other person, as Paul did before Festus and Agrippa?

Did you give witness with dignity and trust, as knowing yourself to be a messenger of the great King?

Act: Write down your answers to these two questions. Think about how your witness could have been better or more effective. Write down the following phrase and complete it with your own words: The next time _____.

Seventh Day: Read Acts 27:1-12.

See: Paul and some other prisoners were placed under the supervision of centurion Julius "of the Augustan Cohort." There was indeed in Caesarea a cohort called "Augusta." It is possible that this centurion belonged to it. On the other hand, there were also some soldiers called "Augustans," who were sent to various parts of the empire on special missions, and therefore it is quite possible that this Julius was an Augustan who had come to Caesarea on some mission and was now returning to Rome.

The ship that the group took was from Adramyttium, which was a city south of Troas. The ship's route took them first to Sidon, where the centurion allowed Paul to visit his "friends." This is the only occasion in which Acts refers to Christians with such a word. Probably the text is quoting the way in which the centurion spoke of Christians, not as Paul's brothers and sisters but as his friends. Most likely Paul visited the Christians there accompanied by a soldier to whom he was chained.

Then, following the north coast of Cyprus, they reached Myra. The text explains that they "sailed under the lee of Cyprus, because the winds were against us." This means that, with the wind blowing from the west, the ship used the island as protection against the contrary wind, while it profited from the direction of the current, which on that coast runs westward.

In Myra they changed to a ship from Alexandria that was going to Italy. Most likely the previous ship continued sailing along the coast of Asia Minor, toward Adramyttium, and that is the reason that the travelers changed ships in Myra. Since this second ship was going from Alexandria to Rome, it would be larger than the previous one. Later, in verse 37, we will be told that there were 276 people aboard.

From the beginning, this second leg of the trip was slow and difficult. The winds were contrary, and the travelers had a hard time reaching Cnidus, on the southwest corner of Asia Minor.

From then on, rather than continuing directly toward the west, which would have been impossible given the direction of the winds, they headed south, in order to sail under the lee of Crete and thus enjoy the protection of that island. Salmone is a cape at the western end of Crete. The city of Lasea, now in ruins, was on the southern coast of Crete, about halfway between the two ends of the island. There is today near those ruins a bay that is still called Kololoiminas, and which is probably what Acts calls "Fair Havens." It is not a good bay, for it is exposed to the wind, and that is why we are told that the place "was not suitable for spending the winter." In verses 9-12 the decision was made not to spend the winter there but to continue to Phoenix. This was a trip of less than forty miles, at the end of which they would be able to anchor in a port that would be well protected from winter winds.

It was already late in the year, and sailing was becoming unsafe. Therefore, all agreed that it would not be possible to reach Italy before the winter, and all that they intended to do now was to find a place to wait for the next sailing season.

There was then a disagreement about what was to be done. Those who had the most experience thought it best to continue west. Paul, on the other hand, told them that they should remain in Fair Havens. Finally the centurion, who apparently was in charge of the decision, listened to the pilot and the owner of the ship and decided that they should sail toward Phoenix.

Judge: This episode may lead us to a brief discussion. It seems very daring on the part of Paul, who was not an expert on sailing, to tell the experts what they should do. However, the rest of the story will show that Paul was right.

Quite often today, when the church seeks to speak a prophetic word on some of the problems debated in the world, it is told to remain silent, for it is the "experts" who really know what is to be done, and the church and those who speak for it are not experts on the subject at hand.

For instance, when the subject of the discussion is environmental pollution and some leaders in the church warn that the practice of doing violence to nature in order to increase profit will eventually resolve in great loss to all, there are attempts to silence them by saying that they are not experts in economy or ecology.

Likewise, when the church or some of its members speak a prophetic word against economic injustice, those who are benefiting from such injustice say that they do not have to listen to what is being said, because after all the prophet is not an economist. Or when the church speaks of the physical harm produced by tobacco, the "experts" in the pay of tobacco companies try to undermine the authority of the church by saying that it is not an expert in health matters and that they are the true experts who know what it best.

Such examples are almost endless. The main point is that in a world in which the experts frequently use their authority to justify evil, it is time for the church to reclaim its authority. That authority is based not on expertise in matters of economy, politics, ecology, or health, but rather on having a clear vision of the future that God has promised—on that central element of the Christian message, the reign of God. Perhaps the church and its members are not "experts," but they have a word from the Lord, and they do have authority.

Act: Take this morning's newspaper and choose a bit of news that refers to a controversial question (for instance, a governmental program against poverty). Divide a page in your notebook into three columns, giving each column one of the following titles: "One Side," "The Other Side," and "Christian Values." Under the first column, list what the experts on one side say. Under the second, list the arguments of the experts who claim the opposite. Under the third, list the things that the church and its members should take into account as they consider the issues being debated.

Go back to the subject under discussion and try to consider everything that is being said in the newspaper under the lens of what you have written in the third column. Write down your reflections. When you have to make up your mind on other subjects of controversy, follow the same method.

For Group Study

Follow the same procedure suggested under "Act," but make the columns on a blackboard or on newsprint. Ask the class to suggest what should be written in each column.

Or take the same bit of news and organize a brief debate about it (with two teams of two or three people each, giving each person two minutes to defend a particular position). Then ask the entire class to point out some things that, as Christians, we should take into account and which the "experts" frequently forget.

W E E K
THIRTEEN

First Day: Read Acts 27:13-26.

See: We are reading a story that is quite frightening for any who have had experience with the sea and its fury. The sailors thought that the south wind was a good sign, so they raised the anchor and went out into the open sea. But immediately they were hit by a strong northeast wind, and with it their difficulties began. With a great deal of effort the sailors were able to recover the small rowboat that apparently they had used to tow the ship out of port. Carried by the wind, they feared that they might hit the rock called Syrtis. For that reason they lowered the sea anchor; but this was not sufficient, and they found themselves forced to lighten the ship by throwing the cargo and eventually even the tackle overboard.

It was then that Paul spoke his words of hope. Beforehand he had warned them not to sail, for their lives would be in danger. But now he told them that they would survive.

Judge: Note that Paul, who at first warned of the difficulties they would have to face, when those difficulties appeared overwhelming, was also the first to announce hope. Similarly the church and its members have to tell the world of the terrible consequences that its decisions may have. But when those consequences arrive, our task is not to make the situation even more desperate; on the contrary, our task is to announce hope.

In our time, we see many of the consequences of sin and injustice, such as poverty, domestic violence, drugs, terrorism, international strife, and so on. In such circumstances, the church has to manifest God's love by speaking words of hope and not only of judgment.

Is this what my church does? Is this what I do?

Act: Make a resolution that throughout today, and into the future, whenever you find somebody who is discouraged, even though it may be as a consequence of his or her own sin, you will speak a word of encouragement and hope. Write down your resolution, so that in reading it again in a few days you may be reminded of it and determine whether you have fulfilled it or not.

Second Day: Read Acts 27:27-38.

See: The difficulties on the high seas continued. One of the reasons we have divided this narrative about the shipwreck is in order to study it during three days so that we may have a clear idea of the time that the travelers spent in doubt and anxiety. (Sometimes we read a text such as this so quickly that we do not realize the length of time to which the text refers.)

Finally, after two weeks of danger, they managed to anchor in an unknown place. It was night. They had no idea where they were. They feared that the sea would drag the ship against the shoals. The sailors tried to flee. Paul and the soldiers prevented them from doing so by casting the boat adrift. Now no one had a way to flee the ship. They were at the edge between disaster and hope. It was then that Paul took bread and encouraged his companions to eat. With that gesture, he restored hope to his anguished companions.

Judge: The church has words of hope for the world. That hope is grounded on the vision that the church has of a different future. However, the world will not believe us if we do not live out of that hope. His fellow travelers believed Paul, and they ate when they saw him eating. The world will believe us, and will be encouraged to believe, by the measure to which it sees us being truly the people of a new hope, a people announcing and already living out of a different future. In the midst of a world in a constant crisis of despair, with overwhelming international tensions, tragic political situations, and an environment ever more polluted, the church has no other alternative than to announce the different future that God has promised, and to do so with its words, with its actions, and with the manner in which it organizes its own inner life.

In our cities, often torn by violence and by poverty, the church has no other alternative than to be a living proof of the hope by which we live. What Paul did reminds us of Communion: He took bread, he gave thanks, he broke it, he invited others to share. Perhaps our task now is to do the same: That our communion be such that we remind the world of the hope of its own salvation, of the reign of God. That in taking bread and sharing it, our very action and the life resulting from it be an announcement of the new order of the reign of God. Such a church is truly hope for the world. The opposite is also true. A church that does not have the necessary faithfulness to be an announcement of hope does not deserve anything else but to be cast out, as Jonah was thrown into the sea from the ship threatened by the storm, or like salt that is good for nothing but being trampled under foot.

Act: Review the various activities of your church. Ask about each of them: Can the neighborhood around my church see hope in this activity or program?

Think of other ways in which your church can be a sign of hope for the community. Write some concrete steps that the church may take. Discuss those steps with other people in the church.

Third Day: Read Acts 27:39-44.

See: By morning, they saw an unknown land with a bay and a beach, and they decided to attempt to bring the ship to the beach. Since time was short and they had no rowboat, they simply cut the anchor cables. The steering oars, which had been tied during the storm, were loosened, and a small sail was raised on the bow, in order to take the ship as close to the beach as possible.

Finally they hit on a shoal (which the Greek text describes as a "place of two seas"). The place on the island of Malta where it has traditionally been thought that Paul and his companions were shipwrecked does indeed have a shoal near the coast. When the bow was finally on the reef, and stuck there, the waves were still battering the stern, and therefore the ship was tearing apart.

The soldiers, who had to answer with their lives if their prisoners escaped, decided to kill them. But the centurion, who seemed to have a growing respect for Paul, forbade it in order to save the apostle. Some swimming, some on boards and other floating objects, eventually all reached the coast.

Judge: The drama of the entire episode is such that we easily lose sight of a surprising dimension of the story: All those who were sailing with Paul were saved by reason of his presence among them. This may seem strange, for we usually think in such individualistic terms that we are convinced that each person is responsible for his or her actions and their consequences. But here God granted Paul the life of all his companions. Thanks to Paul's faithfulness in obeying the mission entrusted to him by God, the rest were also saved.

There is in the Bible a parallel story that moves in the opposite direction. It is the story of Jonah, who takes a ship in order to go in the opposite direction from that in which God wishes to send him. As a consequence of his faithlessness, the entire crew and the ship are in danger, and they eventually have no alternative but to cast him overboard.

It is important to keep these two stories in permanent tension, for while it is true that a faithful church is hope for the world, a faithless church is a threat, and therefore the world may do well to cast it overboard.

Act: The faithfulness of the church is the responsibility of each of its members. Therefore, it is your responsibility. Write the following in your notebook:

Beginning today, rather than criticizing what the church does and does not do, I will do all that I can to make the church more faithful, so that it may be hope to the world.

Then pray, asking for the help of the Holy Spirit in fulfilling the promise.

Fourth Day: Read Acts 28:1-10.

See: The island where the ship wrecked and the passengers found refuge was Malta. To this day the language of the Maltese shows its Phoenician, and therefore Semitic, origin.

Since the shipwrecked were 276, one is to imagine that those gathered around the fire of which verse 2 speaks were just some of them, while others gathered around other fires or found other ways to keep warm. On stormy days in October, the temperature in Malta can easily drop to 54 degrees. Therefore the people who had been shipwrecked, wet as they were, needed to be warmed.

The episode about the snake, short as it is, shows the volatility of people's opinions. First they thought that Paul must be a terrible sinner because the snake bit him. Then, seeing that he did not die, they thought he was a god.

Judge: When we read this story, we see how easily the Maltese changed their opinion regarding Paul. First, when they saw that a snake had bitten him, they were convinced that he was being punished for some great sin. Then, when they saw that the snake's poison did not appear to harm him, they came to the conclusion that he was a god. In both cases, they were mistaken. Paul was neither an exceptional sinner nor a god.

Sadly, the same sort of cheap theology that the Maltese practiced has made its way into the Christian community and is quite popular in some circles. According to that theology, whoever has some misfortune is actually being punished for his or her sin, whereas, on the other hand, whoever has faith and is obedient to God's commandments will be immune from great difficulties and will even prosper economically.

The saddest part of this situation is that such cheap theology turns out to be very expensive. The price we pay for such theology is that we do not dare speak of our sufferings and anxieties, for they are our fault and an indication of our own corruption and lack of faith. The price for such theology is that the poor must internalize their oppression, for they are told that if they are poor it is because of their sin. The price for such theology is a church in which, in contradiction to what is taught in Scripture, the poor, the orphan, and the suffering are shunned, and the rich, the powerful, and the healthy are praised. In short, the price of such theology is abandoning the cross of Christ and its meaning.

Act: Pray: "Teach me, Lord, to recognize you where you are, and not to equate your presence with worldly success or with riches or with health or with power. Teach me above all to see your presence in those who are 'the least,' in whom you come to us: the poor, the hungry, the naked, the widows, the orphans, the suffering."

Fifth Day: Read Acts 28:11-16.

See: Verse 14 is interesting for two reasons. First, it implies that in the relatively small seaport of Puteoli, so far from Palestine, there was already a Christian community. We have no idea how Christianity reached that place, but that in itself serves to remind us that what Acts is telling us is only part of the story. While Paul and Barnabas were carrying on their missionary task, there were apparently many others who also contributed to spreading the gospel.

Second, this verse is interesting because it indicates that Paul had enough freedom to decide to remain in Puteoli for a week at the request of the Christians there. After half a year of constant living together, apparently centurion Julius had come to the point that he not only respected but perhaps even loved the prisoner entrusted to him.

The sojourn of a week in Puteoli gave the believers in that city a chance to send word to Rome, from whence others then left in order to meet Paul and his companions. Some of them, probably the strongest, or perhaps those who were on horseback, met Paul and his companions at the Forum of Appius, which was some forty miles away from Rome. Apparently others met him the next day at a place called Three Taverns. Acts tells us that "on seeing them, Paul thanked God and took courage."

Judge: As a result of our interest in following the events in the life of Paul, or learning exactly what route he took to Rome, quite possibly we have overlooked one of the most surprising elements in this story, which is also the most encouraging: In Puteoli, Paul found believers. From Rome, another group went to the Forum of Appius, and others to the Three Taverns. This encouraged Paul.

One of the marvels of Christian faith is that we have brothers and sisters everywhere in the world. It would be very difficult to find a place so remote and isolated that there are not there some who profess our faith and serve our Lord. In the midst of a world that is constantly bleeding in senseless conflicts and wars, it is urgent for Christians to recover this vision of our close kinship with others throughout the world, thus to promote peace among ourselves and to give the world a message and an example of peace.

Sadly, such has not always been the message of Christians. To this day, in places such as Ireland and the former Yugoslavia, there are Christians of various denominations who hate each other and even kill each other.

What sort of believer are you? What sort of Christianity is taught and practiced in your church?

Act: Resolve to accept anyone who professes faith in Christ as your sister or brother. Do not impose on them measures of orthodoxy, belonging to the same denomination or worshiping in a certain way, or of acting as you think they should. When someone in your church speaks contemptuously of a brother or sister, be it someone in your church or someone in another, rebuke that person lovingly but firmly.

Sixth Day: Read Acts 28:17-29.

See: Despite all the conflicts he had elsewhere with Jewish leaders (not with Judaism itself), the apostle Paul called together the Jewish leaders in Rome. He wanted to let them know what had happened and why he had to appeal to Caesar. They told him that they had received no complaint about him, although they had heard some bad things about Christianity.

A date was determined when they would hear what Paul was teaching, and when that date arrived many gathered. Paul let them know his message, as he had done before in so many synagogues, and the result was essentially the same: some came to believe, and some did not. Apparently addressing more directly those who did not believe, Paul ended his speech with a quotation from Isaiah 6:9-10. On the basis of that quotation, Paul told them that, since they have not believed, it would be the Gentiles who would hear and believe. As in so many other cases, this did not put an end to the matter, and some ancient manuscripts of Acts tell us that they "departed, arguing vigorously among themselves."

Judge: Throughout the book of Acts, as well as in the Gospels, we have seen many miracles and wonders. But those miracles and wonders do not always produce faith in those who see them. Nor is it necessary to see them in order to have faith. What happened in this last chapter of Acts had happened many times before in the same book, and throughout the whole history of the church. Some believe, and some do not. That there be miracles or not is completely secondary. Among these Jewish leaders, as well as among all others who heard Paul at various times, some decided to believe, and some did not.

It is important to remember this, because quite often we imagine that during apostolic times, amid so many miracles, it was easier to believe than it is now. But the truth is that whoever wishes to believe will do so even without miracles. And those who do not believe will not be convinced even by the most astounding miracle.

Those who heard Paul in the first century had to choose between faith and disobedience, whether there were miracles or not. We too have to make a decision between believing and not believing, and whether or not we see miracles around us is secondary. If we see no wonders, we are to believe by faith. If we see miracles galore, we shall still need the same faith in order to believe.

Act: Ask God for faith so that you may believe. Ask not for miracles in order to be convinced. Such a petition is a mere excuse for not believing and especially for not obeying. Simply say: "I believe, help my unbelief."

Seventh Day: Read Acts 28:30-31.

See: With these two verses the book of Acts ends. Here we are told about the manner in which Paul lived in Rome. In Roman times, just as today, one could be arrested and incarcerated in various ways. Paul's situation was similar to our "house arrest," which allows for a certain freedom but still under guard. Paul had the freedom to receive visitors in the house he had rented in Rome. There he continued preaching "with all boldness and without hindrance." These are the last words of the book of Acts.

From other writings and clues we can try to reconstruct what happened to Paul after that. For instance, we hear that Paul eventually reached Spain and that he died in Rome, where he was beheaded under Nero's regime. But Acts does not tell us that. Acts simply stops its story at this point and leaves us with the desire to turn the page and see what happened next.

Judge: Although I have just said that the book ends with these lines, in fact it does not end; or if it ends, it is a very strange ending. Rather than actually finishing its story, the book simply seems to quit. We have spent three months studying the history of the beginnings of Christianity. For some weeks, attention has centered on Paul. We have seen his development from the time when he persecuted Christians to this moment, when it is he who suffers persecution because of his faith. He seems to have reached the high point of his career. He is preparing to appear before the emperor himself. Whoever reads Acts for the first time is looking for the final outcome, but such an outcome is not told. The book simply quits and leaves us, so to speak, in midair. Whatever became of Paul? Acts does not tell us. Whatever became of Peter? Acts does not tell us that either. Whatever became of Philip? Silence.

How are we to explain such an odd ending? Why is it that the author finishes his book without telling us what happened to its main characters? The explanation is simple. The main character in Acts is not Paul, nor is it the apostles or Philip or any other of the seven. What happens to Paul at the end of chapter 28, that is, his disappearing from the scene, has happened before to Peter in chapter 15, and to the others even before.

Luke has written two books: the Gospel of Luke and the book of Acts. The Gospel of Luke tells us about the actions of Jesus. The book of Acts tells us about the actions of the Holy Spirit. In the Gospel of Luke, Jesus is physically present, but he acts by the power of the Holy Spirit. In the book of Acts, Jesus, although physically absent, is still acting and working through the Holy

Spirit. The Gospel of Luke ends with the Ascension. The acts of the Spirit will not end until the Lord returns.

If the book of Acts were only about the actions of Paul and the other apostles, it would be quite interesting as history but would tell us little about our present situation. By now, all the apostles are long dead, and almost twenty centuries stand between them and us. If on the contrary, the book is about the actions of the Spirit, this means that its importance for us is not purely historical. On the contrary, the book of Acts is about ourselves because the actions of the Spirit have not ended, but rather continue among us until the end of time.

In a way it could be said that we—the church that, thanks to the power and presence of the Holy Spirit, continues the work of the apostles—live still in the time of Acts, perhaps in chapter 29. The book contains only twenty-eight chapters, but the Holy Spirit is still writing the history of the people claimed and formed by Jesus, and impelled by the same Holy Spirit. In consequence, all that we have studied during these three months touches us directly. It is not only Paul who was called to preach the gospel in every circumstance. We too are called to do likewise. Sometimes we shall succeed, other times not. Paul and other Christians throughout history had the same experience. Sometimes circumstances are favorable, and everything will seem to smile on us. At other times there will be difficulties everywhere. Paul and all Christians through the ages have also gone through such changing circumstances. Jointly with the apostles, jointly with Paul, jointly with Priscilla and Aquila, jointly with an innumerable company of Christians, we are messengers of Jesus, commissioned by the Holy Spirit.

Act: Review all that you have studied during these three months. Especially read your own notebook. Use a highlighter to mark all that you may have written in your notebook that is still pending. Review all that has been highlighted, and summarize it at the end of your notebook.

With your notebook still open to that summary page, spend some time in prayer, placing before the Lord each of these unfinished tasks or forgotten resolutions, and asking the Holy Spirit for power and guidance so that you may be obedient.

For Group Study

Review with the group what has been studied during the last three months. Especially take each of the main characters in Acts: Paul, Barnabas, Ananias the disciple in Damascus, Philip, Priscilla, Apollos, and Timothy. Assign one of these characters (except Paul, who would take too much time) to a member of the group and ask that person to summarize what Acts says about what eventually happened to his or her assigned figure.

If at all possible, make these assignments two or three days before the group session, so that each participant may look again at Acts to see what the book says about the person assigned to her or him. (This is also another way of inviting them to review what they have studied.)

Suggest to the group what has been said above—that we are living in what could be called Acts 29. Ask the group to discuss what this might mean.

(Remember that when we studied Acts 10–11 we saw that the Spirit works not only for the conversion of those outside, but also for the conversion of the church. Living in Acts 29 does not mean only that we are to have a deep religious life and that we are to witness to our faith as often as possible, but also that our faith has to grow and our character has to be constantly formed and converted by the action of the Spirit.)

To finish the session, invite the group to list the main things they have learned during these three months. Write them down on newsprint. Lead the class in a prayer of gratitude for what you have learned, ending with a petition that the Holy Spirit guide each and all of you.